MW00615982

Rainer Zerbst / Peter Gössel

ANTONI GAUDÍ I CORNET

THE COMPLETE WORKS 1852-1926

GAUDÍ
A LIFE DEVOTED
TO ARCHITECTURE

Half of Barcelona, it is said, was in mourning on 12 June 1926. The funeral procession, which slowly wound its way from the Hospital de Santa Cruz in the old section of Barcelona to the church of the Sagrada Familia, was half a mile long. For two and a half miles, thousands of people lined the streets along the way to pay him their last respects: Antoni Gaudí i Cornet, the "most ingenious of all architects", as his friend and colleague Joaquín Torres-García once said of him, the "most Catalonian of all Catalonians". And indeed, there was hardly a dignitary from his native region who was not among the mourners in the procession.

Gaudí had long held the status of a folk hero. The government instructed that he be laid to rest in the crypt of the as yet unfinished Sagrada Familia, and the Pope granted his approval. It was thus that Gaudí came to rest at the site to which he had devoted the last 43 years of his life; and for the last 12 years it was, in fact, the only site at which he worked. He had created his own homeland, and he was accorded a magnificent funeral.

Just five days before, however, things had looked completely different. He was taking one of his late-afternoon walks – as he did every day after

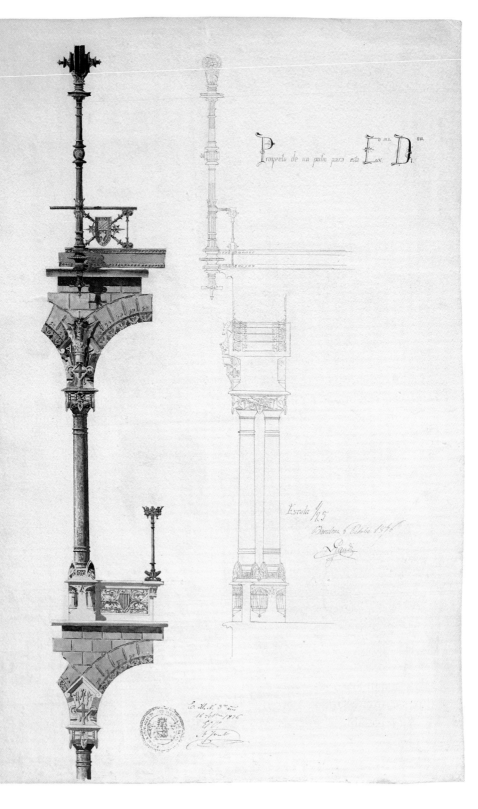

Proyecto de un palo para esta E.^{ma} D.^{on}

Escala 1/25

Barcelona 6 Octubre 1876

PAGE 7 · View of the Nativity
façade of the seemingly
eternally unfinished Sagrada
Familia with its construction
cranes. This was the only
façade that Gaudí was still

able to play a significant personal
role in designing.

LEFT · Gaudí's project for the covered courtyard of the provincial
administration building from his

fourth year of study. What is remarkable here is how he achieved
an aesthetic unity from a variety of
building materials, such as riveted
steel beams, cast iron, masonry
and natural stone.

work – to the San Felipe Neri church to pray; on the way there, he was
hit by a tram and dragged along the street behind it. Gaudí fell to the
ground unconscious. No one, however, recognised the architect who,
although already a famous figure in Barcelona, was hardly ever seen in
public. Taxi drivers refused to transport the shabbily dressed man to the
hospital (for which they were later severely punished). Passers-by then
took pity on the critically injured man and tended to him. A peculiar
end for one of Spain's most renowned architects. And yet this mixture
of contradictions is characteristic of Gaudí's life. For, if Gaudí, in the
end, was celebrated as an outstanding figure by the public and the government, and especially the people, this was not because of his humble
origins, but in spite of them.

He was born in Reus on 25 June 1852 as the son of a coppersmith.
In other words, he was not the product of a particularly affluent environment. Moreover, little Antoni was plagued by illness from an early
age. Rheumatic ailments already prevented him as a child from romp-
ing around on the streets with others his own age. The boy was often
obliged to stay in the house; sometimes he had to be carried by donkey.
His whole life was marked by this affliction: he had to deal with bouts of
rheumatism until he died. The doctors prescribed a strict vegetarian diet
and regular exercise in moderation, which included his customary walks
to the church of San Felipe Neri. And even as a youth Gaudí went on
long walks throughout the area – an unusual pastime in those days.

It is surely fruitless to speculate whether Gaudí would have still taken
his place in Spain's history as the architect he proved to be without his
illness. After all, even if little Antoni could not move about freely, he
was at least able to give his eyes – and his thoughts – free rein. He must

Proyecto de un embarcadero Escala 1/100

ABOVE · As a student, Gaudí put great effort into his design of a boat harbour, making use of various architectural styles. The huge, stretched fabric roofs over the piers remain a defining feature.

PAGE 13 · This group photo was taken at a Gregorian singing course which Gaudí attended.

He can be seen, half-hidden, in the second row.

have been a precocious child who baffled his elders with his amazing insights. When a teacher once pointed out that birds can fly because they have wings, Antoni immediately retorted that chickens in the barnyard also have wings, but only use them to walk. He never lost this sharp eye for detail and the habit of learning from the everyday world around him; indeed, it left its mark on all of his works. His interest in architecture had, incidentally, already come to light when he was a schoolboy in Reus (the school has, of course, been named after him), and at the age of 17 he went to Barcelona to study architecture.

A GENIUS OR A MADMAN?

As a student he lost none of his practical-mindedness: in addition to pursuing his theoretical studies in seminars and at the drawing board, he worked – to earn money – in the offices of several local architects.

He does not seem to have been a particularly good student, but good enough to acquire solid training in the fundamental principles of architecture; his draft of the cemetery gate was marked as "outstanding" and enabled him to pass his examination – though apparently not without some difficulty. But his time at the university was not only revealing in terms of his enthusiasm for architecture; it also showed his strong-minded temperament. In order to give his design-drawing more "atmosphere", he had started by drawing a hearse and, apparently, rendered a much more precise drawing of this carriage than of the subject matter at hand. The professors were not blind to Gaudí's talent for doing things his own way. In the end, there was no doubt in the mind of the chairman of the Faculty for Architecture that this student who had been allowed to pass the examination was either a genius or a madman – an opinion Gaudí was to encounter more than once in the course of his career. For, although he had completed his studies in the proper manner, he soon parted ways with the prevailing rules of architecture.

Gaudí also drew his inspiration from books. He was by no means a revolutionary at the outset of his career. However, the search for a style of his own began in what was an unusually favourable climate for this endeavour. All of European architecture was in flux and receptive to change. There were no fixed, binding norms. The science of history had become established in the 19th century; the previous centuries had become the subject of research in art as well and thus accessible to the young student. The result was an eclecticism which was overwhelming at times.

A number of fashionable trends also contributed to this development. Following the austere Age of Classicism, people were beginning to break out of the corset of strictly applied rules. Romanticism had preached the freedom of feelings and of the subject. This was manifested most clearly in the style of gardens at the time. The era of the symmetrical, neatly trimmed and structured French garden was followed by the blossoming of the English landscape garden. Natural herbage was the maxim. Soon gardens that grew wild were all the rage – or rather, they were planted to look as if they were wild.

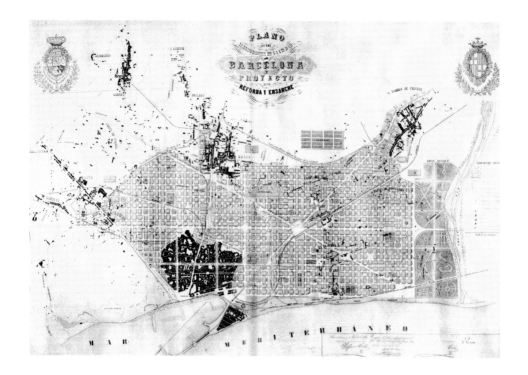

This was accompanied by a veritable fad for the past, the Middle Ages, which not so very long ago had still been defamed as the "dark" ages by the proponents of the 18th-century Enlightenment. The Gothic style underwent a revival – although the term Gothic was applied to anything that bore even the faintest resemblance to the Middle Ages. Palaces were built in the old style, and sometimes even artificial "ruins" were put in the gardens. A strong aversion to rigidly straight lines became widespread, and ultimately gave rise to a mesh of various ornamental lines which would become one of the most fundamental elements of art nouveau.

The Spanish art world was not immune to all this, although the Iberian peninsula, a world unto itself, had always remained somewhat detached from the major trends in Europe. Nevertheless, the writings of the English art theorist John Ruskin were enthusiastically devoured in Spain, and this did not fail to have an effect – even on Gaudí. "Ornament is the origin of architecture", as Ruskin put it in 1853. Three decades later Gaudí would advocate the ornamental in much the same way, and in his own ardent manner. The large iron portals of the Güell Palace, which he designed in Barcelona at the end of the 1880's, could hardly come closer to art nouveau.

THE DANDY

Gaudí also studied the neo-Gothic style propagated above all by French architects. Viollet-le-Duc's book on French architecture from the 11th to the 13th centuries became something like a Bible for young architects, and Gaudí was no exception. He even travelled to Carcassonne, where Viollet-le-Duc had restored the old section of the city. In fact, Gaudí studied the walls so intensively that one of the villagers in the neighbourhood took him for Viollet-le-Duc himself, and paid him his due respects.

The fact that Gaudí could be mistaken for such a prominent figure had to do with his bearing during his early years as a young architect. When one thinks of Gaudí as the shabbily dressed old man who did not necessarily shun publicity but certainly did not seek it either, and did his best to avoid any camera in sight – which is why there are almost no photographs of him – then the image of the young Gaudí provides a startling contrast indeed.

It is true that Gaudí was not exactly blessed with wealth; throughout his studies he lived in rather poor conditions and thus had to earn money on the side; yet he had barely left university before he set out to make up for all the things he had had to forego in previous years, or so it would seem. He developed an unmistakable penchant for a fashionable appearance, for being a dandy – which, by the way, was perfectly in keeping with the times, in which writers such as Oscar Wilde proclaimed that external style and refined, meticulous dress were the highest ideal. And so Gaudí was a magnificent and – for Spain – extraordinary phenomenon. He bought his hats at "Arnau", the foremost hatters; the young architect's calling card (which is on display in the Reus museum today) was carefully designed, and he had his beard tinted with an elegant touch of grey by Audonard, the top hairdressers. Shoes were the only items of clothing he preferred "second-hand". He did not like to wear new shoes because they were uncomfortable, so he had his brother "break them in" for him; practical-minded as he was, Gaudí could be found all around town. How different Gaudí looked as an old man, who at most only took meagre meals and usually got up hungry from the table.

In his heart Gaudí always remained true to his origins. He felt close to the common people. When, after the accident with the tram, people finally recognised who he was, they wanted to move him to a more comfortable room in the hospital, but he insisted: "My place is here among the poor." That certainly is not in keeping with the young Gaudí's preference for high society – though it was of course more a matter of rubbing shoulders with the high society of the mind, i.e. the intellectuals and artists.

BARCELONA AT THE TURN OF THE CENTURY

Barcelona was an enterprising city. The ancient walls had already been torn down in 1854, and the city was bursting on all sides. In the span of only a few years it grew in surface area from approximately 50 acres to more than 500. The population quadrupled during the second half of the 19th century. Thanks to the cotton and iron industries, trade flourished; the upper middle classes had never had it so good. Such developments raised the level of consciousness in the arts as well. The rich liked to surround themselves with artists and writers.

It was not unusual for them all to live under the same roof. This, of course, was an ideal environment for an architect. It is not at all surprising, perhaps, that Gaudí designed nearly all of his buildings for

Barcelona; he seldom had the need to look for other places to work. And this is why a Gaudí fan today need only take a walk through Barcelona to take in all of Gaudí's major works.

The aspiring architect's new social environment naturally affected his way of thinking. He was soon fascinated by the new social theories and ideas. Although he felt at home in intellectual circles, he was also committed to the concerns of workers. It is surely no coincidence that his first major building project was devoted to providing accommodation for factory workers. It was based on collaboration with the Mataró workers' cooperative, an ambitious undertaking reminiscent of the ideas of Robert Owen, the English social reformer who, albeit an industrial magnate himself, zealously worked to improve the living conditions of workers.

The Mataró project was intended to create the architectural prerequisites for such an improvement. Apparently, however, the time was not ripe for such achievements: only a factory hall and a small kiosk were actually built, which somewhat disillusioned the young Gaudí.

Be that as it may, the Mataró project marked the beginning of what was to become growing fame. The project was exhibited at the Paris World Fair in 1878 and led to Gaudí's lifelong friendship with Eusebi Güell i Bacigalupi, for whom he was to design numerous buildings.

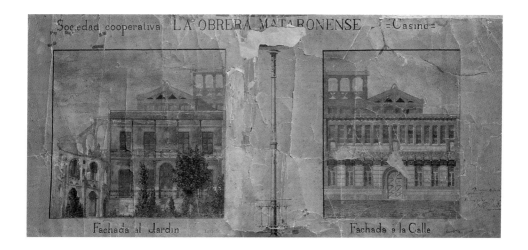

However, that was still in the distant future. For the time being, Gaudí continued to search for his own style, allowing himself to be influenced by the prevailing trends – one of which in particular was neo-Gothic. This, like the workers' project, was not entirely free of political overtones. While it is true that the rediscovery of the Gothic style was a widespread phenomenon of the day in Europe, it held a special attraction for Gaudí's home – Catalonia.

GAUDÍ – A NATIONALIST

Despite the economic boom in Catalonia, and although Catalonia could look back on a glorious past, the political situation of the region was deteriorating. Under Roman rule the country had rapidly grown into a trade centre, and in AD 343 Barcelona was declared a diocese in its own right. During the Middle Ages Catalonia – which was originally called "Gotalonia" after the Visigoths who made Barcelona the capital of their kingdom in the fifth century – was an autonomous county with its own laws and its own language. Modern times – and the emergence of the Spanish Empire under Castilian rule – saw the gradual loss of the region's independence; by the early 19th century, even the use of the Catalonian language had been prohibited in the schools. Thus, for the Catalonians, the late 19th-century revival of the Middle Ages, the discovery of the "Gothic" style, was more than merely a matter of artistic preferences: it became a political signal. Gaudí, too, was caught up in the wave of nationalist sentiment.

Gaudí became a member of the "Centre Excursionists", a group of young men who made pilgrimages to the historical sites of the once glorious past. Gaudí considered himself a Catalonian through and through. He always insisted on speaking Catalonian, even when this meant that his instructions to the workers at the construction sites had to be translated. When, toward the end of his life, he once had to appear in court, he refused to answer in Castilian Spanish.

However, none of these political leanings made Gaudí a partisan to any political program or party. His ties to the people and his homeland were of a more natural and emotional form. His trips to the monuments of the past, therefore, probably had no political significance for him. Rather, he used them to expand his knowledge of the great architectural works of his homeland. These included, in addition to the great Gothic cathedrals – such as Tarragona, only some six miles from his native city of Reus – above all the Moorish structures of Spain's Arabic past. Again Gaudí found himself in good company, and in no small

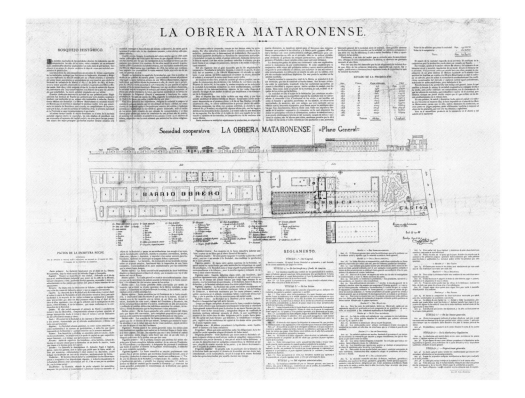

PARA

seccion trasve

For a long time, the Nativity façade was the only façade of the Sagrada Familia whose towers stretched up into the Barcelona sky. The transi-

tion from neo-Gothic architectural elements to Gaudí's later, organi-cally inspired forms was clearly visible on the exposed interior.

numbers at that. While once more lagging behind developments in the rest of Europe, Spain had also been marked by the widespread enthusi-asm for the exotic. In central Europe this fashion of the day had already emerged in the 18th century once the threat of a Turkish invasion had passed – the Turks had been fought off successfully near Vienna in 1688, leaving behind no more than an attraction for what was foreign. The Moorish past had been a part of Spain's history for centuries, and thus the foreign and unusual held less attraction here. However, in the sweep of orientalism which prevailed in the upper-class salons of the 19th cen-tury, the fascination with the exotic began to take hold in Spain as well. The drawing that Gaudí submitted for the entrance examination at the university is already faintly reminiscent of Moorish façades, although it brings to mind the large domes of the Italian Renaissance.

INITIAL ATTEMPTS

Gaudí never cared much for purity of style. He never made exact imi-tations, but preferred to draw inspiration from the buildings of the past. He thus kept completely to the teachings of Viollet-le-Duc, who had warned against the uncritical adoption of old models; as he saw it, the great works of the past were there to be analysed as a source of new insights which would help to create a style of architecture for the present. Gaudí's work seems to be the realisation of this theoreti-cal program (and Viollet-le-Duc's "reconstruction" of the old section of Carcassonne is in many respects also new and therefore more than a mere "reproduction"). The mixture of different architectural styles in the work Gaudí prepared for his entrance examination may have been

People out on a stroll enjoy the view of the city from the promenade in Park Güell in 1936. Flower boxes on natural stone columns line the path, which Gaudí intended to guide visitors not only physically, but also spiritually away from the heat of the city.

INTRODUCTION

the very reason why he was given only a "pass" mark, the lowest grade awarded by the university. The year before, a project that was similarly fantastic in nature had also failed to earn him the special prize he had hoped for.

Official recognition in the form of prizes was never forthcoming for the duration of Gaudí's life. Perhaps this is the reason why Gaudí always felt that he had failed in his work, or at least why he often made remarks to that effect. Apparently his architectonic ideas were too daring to win the acknowledgement and praise of the governmental or municipal authorities. Only once was he awarded a prize – and, as one might expect for one of his most conventional works: the Casa Calvet. But then his work was seldom commissioned by "public authorities". Only at the beginning of his career did he have an opportunity to work for the city, a relatively small project: in February 1878 the city of Barcelona commissioned the "young and industrious architect D. Antonio Gaudí" to design a streetlamp; the project was carried out, and well received by both the press and the general public. Other than that, however, most of Gaudí's work was done at the desk and for the desk – plans, projects which, with few exceptions, never materialised; they included, among other things, a massive desk which looked like a small building that Gaudí designed for himself. However, the design has not survived.

Despite the lack of official public recognition for Gaudí, there was no lack of recognition for his work from other sources: private patrons who recognised his genius were always present in his life. After he had finished his first larger-scale projects, he was swamped with orders. Interestingly enough, he received his most important commission even before he had become known among the general public. He had not yet commenced work on his first spectacular projects – the Casa Vicens, the country house El Capricho and especially the Güell Palace – when he was entrusted with the design of one of the most ambitious architectural undertakings in Barcelona. In 1881 the "Asociación Espiritual de Devotos de San José" (Association of the Worshippers of St Joseph) had bought up a whole block of houses situated on what was then the city limits of Barcelona. A church for the adoration of the Holy Family (Sagrada Familia) was to be built on this piece of land.

The project was not free of political considerations. It was to be an expression of protest against increasing industrialisation, against the loss of old values. St Joseph had been elevated in the 19th century to the status of the patron saint of those movements within the Catholic Church which called for a reaction to its increasing secularisation. The reference to the family was an appeal for a return to traditional values. In other words, the point was not merely to have a church building, but to surround the church with an entire complex of social facilities: schools, workshops, meeting rooms – a church-sponsored project on the same scale as that of the Mataró workers, on which Gaudí had worked so intensively shortly before.

However, nobody was thinking of Gaudí at this point; he was still too young and unknown. The architect Francisco de Paula del Villar y Lozano, for whom the young Gaudí had already worked as a student – particularly on the Montserrat church – was commissioned to design the project. Villar submitted a model in the neo-Gothic style and began with the excavation of the crypt. Subsequently, however, del Villar fell out with the Association and withdrew from the project. One can only speculate as to why Gaudí, of all people, was then entrusted with the responsible post. Perhaps it had something to do with his collabora-tion on the church in Montserrat, but also perhaps with the architect Joan Martorell i Montells. It was the latter who was first approached to continue with the work on the building, as he was, after all, the leading representative of the neo-Gothic style in Catalonia. However, Martorell declined. Gaudí had worked with him in the early 1880s, creating works composed entirely of a combination of neo-Gothic and elements of the Spanish ceramics tradition. Perhaps these samples of his work were the deciding factor: in any case, on 3 November 1883, Gaudí became Villar's successor and thus embarked on an architectural project which would occupy him for the rest of his life and to which he devoted himself exclusively in the last years of his life.

Up to this point, Gaudí had still had to prove himself as an archi-tect. However, the order from the Association of the Worshippers of St Joseph appears to have been the first step in what was to become a rising career. For, it was followed, in the very same year, by commissions

ABOVE · A herd of goats roams the still barren landscape near the Sagrada Familia. In 1915, when this photo was taken, this area of Eixample had not yet been built on.

FOLLOWING SPREAD · The exception: an already completed school building surrounded by a wall. In the background are the apse towers of the Sagrada Familia.

for two major projects. Gaudí broke new ground in architecture with his very first work.

The brick manufacturer Manuel Vicens i Montaner had already taken Gaudí under contract to construct a residence in 1878. Work on the project began in 1883 in the Calle Sant Gervasi in Barcelona (today the Calle de les Carolines). It is difficult to identify the elements of any particular style in this work, and any attempt to do so requires constant re-thinking. The building is not particularly original in terms of the floorplan. Its appeal derives rather from the design of the outer façade and its interior. A Moorish influence is unmistakable. Small towers, reminiscent of the minarets on mosques, decorate the roof. Delicately fashioned tile patterns create the impression of the filigrain lattice patterns on Moorish buildings. The ornamental impression of the tiled walls is repeated in the interior. Yet this is not an imitation of Arabic architecture, which only served as a source of inspiration for Gaudí to create his own ornamentation. It would therefore be more appropriate to speak in terms of Mudejar rather than of a Moorish style. (Mudejar was a mixture of Spanish and Arabic architecture). The smoking room comes closest to a purely Moorish style.

THE 'MOORISH' PERIOD

But the most intriguing aspect of this work is the mixture of materials Gaudí used in the building, combining unfinished rubble with ceramic tiles. This mixture of ornamental-looking tiles and cheap stone is a recurring feature in his work. And this, Gaudí's first great architectural achievement, is revealing of his style in still another respect: it took five

years to complete. In other words, Gaudí's "organic" style of architecture, in which one idea leads to another, had already begun to evolve at this early date. Of course, the costs involved nearly drove Gaudí's sponsor to the brink of bankruptcy. However, he was richly compensated in the years to come: Gaudí's use of ceramic tiles initiated a veritable wave of fashion in Catalonia, and Vicens manufactured large quantities of these tiles.

Gaudí was engaged in construction work on a country house in Comillas, near Santander, at the same time as the Casa Vicens, and while the two are similar in style, the former was considerably more imaginative. Here, too, the foundations are made of undressed stone. But the walls are richly decorated with coloured tiles. The Moorish influence is even stronger in this work. A slender tower rises up like a minaret, with a "lid" on top – Gaudí's idea. But if one takes a closer look, one will see that it only appears to be Moorish and that the pattern of the tiles is totally European: a blossom that looks like a sunflower. This theme is a recurrent feature, and indeed its repetition also points to principles of Arabic architecture where repetition plays a predominant role. There is nothing uniform about this structure. It is thus deserving of its name: "El Capricho" – a caprice, a whim. It is not the only house designed by Gaudí that was given a nickname. People also liked to call the Casa Milà "La Pedrera" – the quarry – and not without reason. For the time being, however, Gaudí's work was dominated by Moorish elements, although it cannot be said for certain, even in the case of an early work such as El Capricho, whether the tower is patterned after Arabic or Persian models.

While the projects in Comillas and Barcelona were still in progress, a strong friendship developed that was to influence his development as an architect for almost as long as his work on the Sagrada Familia in Barcelona. During the Paris World Fair, in which Gaudí's projects were also exhibited, he attracted the attention of a man whose personality was very similar to that of the young architect: Eusebi Güell.

GÜELL – GAUDÍ'S GREAT PATRON
Güell was a typical representative of the new Catalonia. Brick-manufacturing had made him a wealthy man; travels to England had

ABOVE · In addition to the numerous colourful buildings, the external uniformity of the brickwork at the Bishop's Palace in Astorga is remarkable. However, Gaudí did not complete the building himself.

PAGE 36 · Its guided lighting and spatial layout transform the modest Colegio Teresiano into a masterpiece whose strengths lie within.

exposed him to new currents in art as well as to innovative ideas on social reform. It was not long before Gaudí became a welcome guest at the Güell house, where the doors were always open to artists. Perhaps it was in Güell's library that Gaudí first became familiar with the influential writings of John Ruskin and William Morris. In any case, he was exposed for the first time to preliminary forms of art nouveau during the evenings at the house, as poetry written by the Pre-Raphaelites, especially that of Dante Gabriel Rossetti, was often read on such occasions. This movement, both painters and poets, had advocated a return to the Middle Ages and aspired to freedom from the strict classicistic rules of art, especially through the use of rich ornamentation. In 1910, Güell was made a baron, but even before that, Gaudí saw him as the embodiment of nobility. Genuine nobility, as he once put it, is manifested in heightened sensitivity, immaculate conduct and the proper social standing. He discovered all of these in Güell, who, for his part, had met his ideal in Gaudí: the combination of artistic genius and social commitment.

As early as 1883 Gaudí designed a hunting pavilion for Güell in Garraf that bore the same elements as the Casa Vicens and El Capricho – a combination of unfinished stone and tiles. It was never built. Then, in 1884, Gaudí redesigned Güell's estate in Barcelona. Here again, the Moorish influence can be encountered, with the standard miniature towers above the riding hall, for example. However, signs of new trends also appear. The garden-gate indicates that Gaudí had apparently already begun to incorporate elements of art nouveau from the north, and the interior of the horse stables – now the location of the Gaudí professorship at the Technical College of Architecture – reveals those unmistakable neo-Gothic elements that Gaudí would develop to perfection in the years to come.

Initial results of this new direction can be seen in his first major project for Güell. In 1886 Gaudí began with the manufacturer's large residential home in Barcelona, expanding it into a veritable palace. Here, Gaudí's eccentric style became manifest in full-fledged form. Instead of beginning with fixed plans for the building's construction, he worked on the design as he went along. Just as in nature, where plants undergo changes as they grow, so Gaudí's buildings, too, were the products of a gradual process. A small music room was originally to be set up on the periphery of the building for Güell, a lover of Wagner. However, this music room must have become so fascinating with each new phase of the construction process, that it was eventually moved back into the centre of the building until it spread out over more than three floors. The palace, which also has a kind of "underground car park" for horse carriages and a genuine "forest" of richly decorated, odd-looking chimneys, proved to be truly fantastic, a product of the imagination, despite the historical elements of style which always shine through: numerous metal art nouveau ornaments as well as pointed arches reminiscent of Gothic architecture.

THE 'GOTHIC' PERIOD

The two other structures that originated in those years were much more austere, more "Gothic" in nature, and it is no coincidence that they served religious purposes. With respect to the school of the Order of St Theresa in Barcelona, the Colegio Teresiano, Gaudí's task was confined to the upper floors, as the building was already under construction at the time. The building exhibits forms which are quite strict – one might say, neo-Gothic in its purest form, albeit in Gaudí's special rendition. For already as a student Gaudí had learned from his great model, Viollet-le-Duc, that the structures of the past could at best serve as sources of inspiration and should never be imitated. This corresponded entirely to Gaudí's own views; he found Gothic architecture fascinating, but also flawed, especially with regard to design.

Gaudí saw the flying buttresses – an indispensable component of Gothic architecture – purely as aids to bear the weight of the arches. He referred to them derisively as "crutches". He wanted to manage without crutches. The first indications of this are to be found in the soaring parabolic arches used in the upper halls of the Colegio Teresiano. By contrast, the massive façades of a residence Gaudí later designed in León, with rough walls interrupted by numerous pointed arched windows, looks like something taken from the Middle Ages, as does the large Bishop's Palace in Astorga. However, the design of the Colegio Teresiano

already alludes to the element that Gaudí devised to overcome the "flaws" of Gothic design, i.e. the slanted pillars.

This endeavour took up all of Gaudí's energy, particularly as he was then proceeding with work on the Sagrada Familia – a task which he did in his spare time, as it were. There was hardly time for private life. He never married, although he was on the verge of doing so at least twice in his life. He later claimed that he had never felt the urge to marry. However, had the young American woman whom he happened to meet on one of his excursions to look at cathedrals not already been engaged, perhaps Gaudí would not have remained a bachelor. It is said that she preoccupied his thoughts for years after their meeting. At the age of 32 – or so it is said – he even went so far as to become engaged, although this is based on hearsay. In any case, one senses here the extent to which Gaudí lived for his architecture. He would have found little time for private matters.

THE ROAD TO A STYLE OF HIS OWN

After this brief interlude of works during which Gaudí followed a strict, more or less Gothic style, he immersed himself completely in developing his own style. Apart from the occasional reference to art nouveau, all imitative elements gradually disappeared from his work. This may be the most distinctive and possibly the only outstanding aspect of the residence he constructed in 1898 for the heirs of Pere Màrtir Calvet in Barcelona – a house which marks the beginning of Gaudí's exclusive concentration on "his" city, on Barcelona. He had never travelled much anyway, except for a few study trips. Otherwise he concentrated his efforts on Santander, León (the Bishop's Palace in Astorga and the Casa Botines) and, of course, on Barcelona. The reconstruction of the Cathedral of Palma de Mallorca was a prominent exception, albeit an intriguing project. In this "major work" of Spanish neo-Gothic architecture, Gaudí moved the choir stalls from the main nave to the altar. This enhanced the soaring effect of the Gothic interior – a task that must have been especially fascinating for Gaudí, who was so intensely preoccupied with the principles of Gothic architecture.

PAGE 39 · An important component of Gaudí's plans for the restauration of the Palma Cathedral was making the high altar visible to the congregation again. Instead of a crucifix and an altarpiece, an opulently designed canopy elevates the freestanding Mensa Domini.

ABOVE · From 1906 until his death, Gaudí lived in the unsold show home for the planned housing development in Park Güell. It was built by Francesc Berenguer i Mestres in the Modernismo style.

ABOVE · The appearance of the balcony balustrades at the Casa Batlló gave rise to all manner of comparisons, yet how they were made is also interesting.
They began with original-sized plaster models from the Sagrada Familia workshop. They were then produced from cast iron; the openings were closed with riveted flat iron bars.

PAGE 45 · Reminiscent of a Doric temple, the planned market hall beneath the large square of Park Güell features large mosaic medallions in place of some columns.

PAGE 46 · The original ceiling lamp in the living room of the Casa Batlló has since been relocated. However, it was not designed by Gaudí himself. The lamp shown here was installed at a later point in time.

Gaudí had made a name for himself in designing churches; his students (who were also fervent admirers) spread the word. The Casa Calvet and Casa Botines had given him practice in constructing residences. Yet he still had another important new discovery to make. And again it was Eusebi Güell who provided him with the opportunity and helped him to obtain yet another contract.

Gaudí received nearly all of his commissions through private contacts. He would in all likelihood not have been awarded the contract to design the Bishop's Palace in Astorga if it had not been for the influence of Bishop Joan Baptista Grau i Vallespinós, who had been in Tarragona before he was called to Astorga, and had known Gaudí for quite a long time; he, too, was a native of Reus. Grau died while the palace was still being constructed, and there were immediate differences of opinion between the architect and the episcopal administration. Gaudí withdrew from the project. His successor changed the building plans – and the structure collapsed several times as a result. Gaudí's designs did not lend themselves easily to change.

A PARK IN THE ENGLISH STYLE

Gaudí's sphere of influence was expanded by means of an ambitious, new project initiated by Güell. Güell had found himself quite taken by the gardens in England, and wanted to create something similar in Barcelona. Gaudí was to create a garden city in complete harmony with the countryside. In the end, only two of the buildings originally planned for the project were actually made. Güell Park is one of Gaudí's numerous unfinished works.

But the park itself is more significant than the two villas that were built; it became an architectural work in its own right, and one of unusual daring. Above all, it is the first major work that fully and completely transformed the imagination of Gaudí – now an architect in his mature period – into reality. Although the plans were incomparably more ambitious than one might guess when viewing the finished results, the latter demonstrate that Gaudí nevertheless burst the mould of all previous architectural practices. The structures –

especially the huge terrace in the centre – are audacious in shape. The design of the surfaces and edges attests to a freedom which even today is hardly matched.

With this project, Gaudí for the first time put his comprehensive concept of the architect's profession into practice. Even the person whose theories he adhered to most, John Ruskin, had advocated that the architect present a synthesis of the arts; the architect had to be both painter and sculptor. Gaudí united all of this in one person. The endlessly long bench, decorated with ceramic tile fragments, which runs through the park in the form of a snake, has the effect of a colourful painting by Joan Miró. Gaudí uses the ceramic fragments to construct an almost surrealistic painting, a three-dimensional painting in the very midst of the countryside, if you will. From thence on he knew no bounds. He unwaveringly gave his architectonic fantasies full rein; these are, after all, anything but pure figments of the imagination, based as they are on a strict constructional principle.

Although he then turned his attention to the design of two residential complexes, Gaudí nevertheless created something entirely new in this area. From 1904 to 1906 he designed a residence at 43, Paseo de Gracia in Barcelona that was completely innovative. Whereas Güell Park revealed the overflowing imagination of an architect quite drunk with colours, the Casa Batlló showed him to be an architect who was diverging ever further from architecture as an artificial creation of the human hand. The greenish-blue sheen of the façade evokes the surface of the sea, crowned with little peaks of foam. The window sills and frames seem to have been moulded out of clay. The façade – although tightly inserted between the two soberly designed houses on either side – has been set into motion. Everything seems to be welling up and then receding. The roof, with its multitude of chimneys, looks like a miniature version of Güell Park. Central heating was not common in Barcelona, as each room was usually heated individually; this gave Gaudí the opportunity to put an array of capricious chimneys atop the roofs.

The population was dumbfounded. They had never seen the likes of this before. The house defied any form of classification. The

amazement was even greater in response to his second major project, at No. 92 in the same avenue. This was not merely another case of Gaudí designing a relatively small house wedged into a row of other houses, but a huge corner house.

Unlike the Batlló house, the façade is totally devoid of colour. However, the bulging effect is more intense. The protruding rounded oriel windows cling to the façade like honeycombs. The building as a whole is a single mass of backward and forward movement. One is reminded of the cave dwellings cut into the sides of mountains by African tribes – or of the catacombs of St Peter embedded into the Salzburg hill. The flowing movement continues into the interior. With this work Gaudí reached the pinnacle of his organic style of architecture: the building seems to have grown naturally, and it does not involve the customary use of bricks or carrying walls. The house is more like a huge sculpture than a house in the conventional sense of the word.

HIS LIFE'S WORK

If the public had been taken aback by the Casa Batlló – the Casa Milà caused an uproar. At a loss for words, all they could do, apparently, was resort to irony. Numerous parodies appeared in the newspapers; nicknames such as "the quarry", "the pâté" and "the hornets' nest" replaced the serious-sounding name "Milà" (the client who commissioned the work, Pere Milà i Camps).

In view of this seemingly inexhaustible store of architectural imagination, it should not be forgotten that Gaudí was unceasingly preoccupied with the Sagrada Familia project. It was still not completed when Gaudí died. However, Gaudí was fully aware of the significance of what he had set out to accomplish. He considered himself as being in the great tradition of mediaeval cathedral architects.

A cathedral is not the work of a single architect, but of several generations. St Joseph himself will complete it, Gaudí used to say, not only because the project was ambitious in scope, encompassing not merely a church, but a small community. It also had something to do with the founders' resolution, which required that the church be funded exclusively through donations and tithes – a church of the poor. It was not unusual for Gaudí himself to go around collecting money to continue the construction work. After 1914 he did not take on any new work, but devoted himself exclusively to work on the cathedral. He eventually took up quarters in the workshop on the building site. As was his custom, he always discussed the project with the workers. As a result, many changes were made over the years.

One could write a book about the Sagrada Familia's design. It is a synthesis of Gaudí's creative impulses. The overly high, parabolically shaped arches are repeated in the design of the gigantic, slender soaring towers. The bizarre spires of the four towers on the façade devoted to the birth of Christ reveal the same use of loud colours characteristic of Güell Park. The church was supposed to be colourful in any case. Gaudí always said that nature is not monochromatic. Whenever someone praised the nice sandy brown of the undressed stones used in the façade, he retorted laconically, "It's going to be painted over."

Above all, Gaudí used this church to develop his theory of how the Gothic style could be perfected. There are no supporting pillars or flying buttresses. His design concept of the slanted pillars stood the test of time. He had used these pillars most effectively in a crypt he designed for his friend Güell, who required it for his workers' settlement on the outskirts of Barcelona.

When Gaudí died so tragically in 1926, he left behind an unfinished opus. Perhaps this is in keeping with the spirit of his architecture, which worked less with fixed structures, but was increasingly patterned after nature. Gaudí did not bequeath us a polished theory, but only insights, which, however, go further than many a well-built model. He had no successors. His work could not be carried on. Whenever other architects assumed work on projects he had already begun, they betrayed Gaudí's original intentions, and as a result, the buildings he had so carefully designed did not last for very long. The Bishop's Palace in Astorga collapsed several times, whereas the vaulted wood construction of Gaudí's first major project – the factory hall of Mataró – has stood the test of time.

AN ARCHITECTURAL GENIUS

It is difficult to speculate as to all the things that Gaudí could have done had he had modern materials such as reinforced concrete. On the other hand, he might even have rejected them. He refrained for the most part from using cement, for example, even though this construction material would certainly have been available to him. He preferred to build his pillars out of bricks. While his structures may appear rather extravagant, and the surface may look expensive as it shines in the sunlight from the south, Gaudí preferred to use everyday materials, and always went back to the great craftsman's tradition of his home town: ceramics and smithery.

He created veritable wonders out of the simplest materials. Perhaps nature served as his model here, as it did in so many other ways. He departed ever further from the artificiality of building, coming ever closer to nature. "Do you want to know where I found my model?",

An historical model of the Sagrada Familia. Models were an important element in Gaudí's design process, and he had numerous models made with various dimensions, including some 1:1 models for parts of the sculptural design of the façades.

INTRODUCTION

LEFT · Gaudí made static models of his vaults by hanging small sacks of shot pellets attached by strings or chains to them. The weight of these was chosen to mimic the expected load. This

reproduction of the model of the Church of Colonia Güell in Santa Coloma de Cervelló is turned upside down, to make the dome construction more coherent.

PAGE 53 · Photos of the hanging model in turn assisted Gaudí when sketching the outer shape, as shown here, as well as for the Church of Colonia Güell.

he once asked a visitor to his workshop. "An upright tree; it bears its branches and these, in turn, their twigs, and these, in turn, the leaves. And every individual part has been growing harmoniously, magnificently, ever since God the artist created it." In the nave of the Sagrada Familia, Gaudí designed a veritable forest of pillars which branch out and upward in many directions.

When Albert Schweitzer visited the church, Gaudí explained his approach by referring to the tired, plodding donkey who brings the Holy Family to Egypt: "When it became known that I was looking for a donkey as a model for the Flight to Egypt, they brought me the most beautiful donkey in Barcelona. But I couldn't use it." He finally found the donkey he was looking for hitched to the wagon of a woman selling scouring sand. "Its head was hanging down, almost touching the ground. With a great deal of effort I was able to persuade the woman to bring it to me. Then, after the donkey had been covered, section by section, with plaster, she wept because she thought that it would not survive. That was the donkey for the Flight to Egypt, and it makes an impression on you because it is not invented, but real."

It is this affinity with nature that also ultimately distinguishes Gaudí from the art nouveau artists with whom people like to associate him. The ornamental strain in art nouveau is based on natural forms, but remains purely ornamental, and above all two-dimensional, purely linear. For Gaudí, however, nature consisted of forces that work beneath the surface, which was merely an expression of these inner forces. For example, he studied how stone blocks behaved when placed under great pressure by putting them in a hydraulic press: the stones did not burst or fissure from top to bottom, but expanded in the middle – a phenomenon which, as Gaudí believed, had already been recognised by the Greeks, who made their pillars a bit stronger in the middle than at the ends.

Gaudí was a pragmatist. Unlike other architects of his time, he did not work at a drawing board. He was always present at the construction site, talking things over with the workers, thinking things over, making a draft, rejecting an idea. His drawings look like impressionist sketches, and not at all like design drawings.

Gaudí experimented before he built. In preparing the daring arch designs in the Güell Colony church, he devised a model out of strings, from which he suspended small sacks of sand, corresponding to the weight which the supporting arches and pillars would have to carry. This served as an "upside-down" model of sorts: a picture of it had only to be turned upside down to get a clear idea of what the final structure would look like. This procedure is not at all uncommon today, decades after this first experiment. The workers often asked how something was going to hold up; but it did. Looking at the dressing table designed by Gaudí for the Güell Palace, one is prompted to ask the same question.

Gaudí's works could never have been designed solely on the drawing board. This was not only because of the organic-looking spatial design, but also Gaudí's specific feel for space. Gaudí's aspiration was to depart from conventional walls. His ideal of a house was an organic body that seemed to live in and of itself. He always went back to his origins, to the profession of his ancestors in his spatial designs. A smith was a man who could create a body from sheet metal. This called for imagination. Before he could begin working, the smith had to imagine a hollow space. Gaudí's best structures are such hollow spaces. This approach was so different to that of, say, Mies van der Rohe, who worked with clearly defined surfaces and walls as basic elements. It is characteristic that van der Rohe's father was a stonemason, a man, in other words, who did not create a hollow body out of flat material, but instead took something away, broke something off a solid body.

Gaudí's pragmatic approach also had its disadvantages, of course. He was not a theoretician; above all, he did not create a school in the strict sense. And, with the exception of a few works from his early years,

ABOVE · The view from one of the Apostle Towers in 1936 shows how the city was increasingly concentrating around the church, which had been situated in an open field when construction began.

PAGE 57 · The days of the construction cranes, which were an indispensable part of the Sagrada Familia for such a long time, seem to be numbered. The building's mark on the skyline as well as its interior have become iconic, with only the completion of the building works remaining before it reaches full maturity.

PAGE 58/59 · The large number of visitors to the cathedral's interior are kept in check by today's elaborate visitor management system.

he left no written documents. Most quotations attributed to Gaudí are based on hearsay. Moreover, soon after his death, Gaudí's style receded into the background of discussion. Bauhaus, with its functionally oriented style, set the tone of the day, and its fundamental features contradicted those of Gaudí's.

ARCHITECTURE OF THE FUTURE

There was, of course, no doubt in Gaudí's mind that his architecture would have implications for the future. When asked whether the Sagrada Familia was one of the great cathedrals, he replied: "No, it is the first in an entirely new series." However, this prophecy has yet to be fulfilled. But even though Gaudí's influence waned during the first half of the 20th century, his significance for the Catalonian movement remained unchanged. When, in 1925, a scholar questioned the significance of Gaudí the architect, he unleashed a storm of protest and a heated debate which raged in the press for four months.

It would seem particularly suitable, considering the times in which we live today, to contemplate intensively the essence of Gaudí's architecture.

Our situation is not so very different from that of 100 years ago, when Gaudí developed his art. We, too, have turned away from the grey façades, the all too clear-cut, sober lines. Although we have not as yet witnessed a direct and radical reaction comparable to that of art nouveau, Gaudí's comment on his Casa Batlló could almost be taken as a prophecy for the very near future: "The corners will vanish, and the material will reveal itself in the wealth of its astral curves; the sun will shine through all four sides, and it will be like a vision of paradise."

The voices heard today do not sound so very different. On the occasion of the international crafts trade fair held in Munich in 1974, Josef Wiedemann praised Gaudí's work with the following words: "His structures are soothing oases in the wasteland of functional buildings, precious gems in the uniform grey of the lines of houses, creations pulsating with melodic rhythm in the dead mass of their surroundings."

Gaudí's work remained but a torso. The Sagrada Familia is almost symbolic of this. It is more than just an example of Gaudí's magnificent architectonic and religious vision – it transports his work as a phenomenon that continues to live and have an effect into our present. Even if the building can be completed for the 100th anniversary of Gaudí's death, this will not mark the end of all work to be done on the cathedral and its furnishing – because how can a living building as Gaudí imagined it ever reach a final point of conclusion? Work on the western façade alone took 30 years. When Gaudí died, he left behind no more than the beginnings of an architectural work which existed rather more in his imagination than in reality. Shortly after Gaudí's death in July, 1926, Kenji Imai came from Japan to look at various underground stations in Europe. His impression of the Sagrada Familia reflects more the fragmentary status than the vision of a completed work: "The façade of the transept on the north-east side and the vaulting wall on the north-west side were finished, but not the dome. In other words, one could see up into the grey sky ... The parabolic, 300-foot-high bell towers stood in pairs over the three gables as if they formed a cave of stalactites. The scaffolding reached up to the top of the towers. The word 'Hosanna' was sculpted into the colossal stone, winding its way around the high towers ... I took leave of the temple on that rainy day with a very heavy heart ..."

CASA VICENS

Calle de les Carolines, Barcelona

One can hardly imagine a more extravagant debut for a young architect. It rises before one like a fairytale castle from *Arabian Nights* at 24, Calle de les Carolines in Barcelona. And yet in reality, it is quite a small house, and not even the home of a prince, but the residence of a brick and tile manufacturer. Ten years passed between the building being contracted and its completion. But proper work was done on it for only five years – surely not a long time in view of the result. It unites the Spanish bourgeois tradition (which it achieved with amazingly cheap stone) and the centuries-old Arabic tradition. Gaudí made something quite unique out of the building, beginning in a more or less Spanish vein at the bottom and becoming increasingly Arabic towards the top, perhaps even Persian – it is difficult to distinguish between the two.

PAGE 61 · From the frontage on Calle de les Carolines, it is barely noticeable that the right-hand section with two balconies was a later addition, built in 1925 in the style of Gaudí by Joan Baptista Serra de Martínez. Gaudí himself checked the drawings before work was carried out. At one time, the protruding corner tower was the subject of much discussion, as the architects' contemporaries questioned its stability.

LEFT · This overview must have been taken after 1925. The conservatory is without the folding shutters, which were added recently. Part of the railings were later removed to make way for new buildings.

In fact Gaudí had already met Manuel Vicens, the stockbroker and supporter of the Catalan Renaissance movement, some time before. It was in 1883 that the architect first submitted designs for the famous house in Barcelona bearing its owner's name. It then took another five years for construction to be completed. Vicens owned a house in Alella where Gaudí spent one or two summers, working on his drawings for the local parish church, and his friend's commission would certainly have been discussed. When Gaudí began building the structure in 1883, in other words with quite some delay, he had only worked on publicly funded buildings. Designing a residence was new territory for him. Moreover, the task was not exactly an easy one. The house had to be built on a plot of land which was not particularly large, and was set in a row of rather conventional-looking buildings.

In terms of its architectonic structure, this Gaudí residence is not very striking, either. Compared with the complex spatial structures characteristic of his later works, this house would even seem dull. The two storeys are divided up fairly equally, owing to the continuous line of the main walls. The foundation is more or less rectangular; apart from the covered porch leading to the dining room, which juts out slightly. And yet the Casa Vicens already attested to Gaudí's talent as an architect who combined imagination with originality. Above all, it is an early example of Gaudí's practical bent despite all his predisposition for the bizarre. For example, he situated the building at the very rear of the site, leaving the garden in one piece, making it seem much larger than it actually was.

The rectangular form of the foundation is thus already somewhat disguised. The extravagant decoration of the plain façade with numerous little protruding gables and the design of the outer surface of the

walls provide an added touch. These walls look like small gems, although Gaudí used quite simple materials. The basis is an undressed ochre-coloured stone – of the sort Gaudí frequently used in later works – combined with rough bricks. This contrast is of itself intriguing. His rather ordinary brickwork dons the appearance – when set against the roughly chiselled undressed stone – of decorative stone. However, the outside of this house draws its fascination from the lavish use of coloured ceramic tiles which, on the one hand, seem to run like supports through the walls, and on the other, are arranged in the form of a chessboard pattern. These geometric ornaments, when viewed from a distance, are reminiscent of Arabic structures, although it must be said that one cannot yet precisely discern from this early work whether or not the pattern might be Persian. Here Gaudí was already playing with ornaments. Upon closer examination one can also make out indigenous elements: numerous tiles are painted with the luminescent orange marigolds that were growing all over the garden. And the small towers decorating the roof vaguely remind us of Moorish structures, but, more probably, it recalls an Arabian-style pavilion that stood in Parc de Montjuïc at the time. In the mid-19th century, a blend of a romanticised, neo-Moorish style and neo-Gothic predominated in this part of Spain. The Spanish pavilion at the 1878 World's Fair in Paris was built along similar lines. On the other hand, what was genuinely new was Gaudí's increasing use of motifs from the world of nature, and not only as decoration. For example, dwarf palm leaves became a basic element in the design of the wrought iron railings. The Casa Vicens is a collage of highly varied styles. If this house has one distinguishing characteristic, it is that of an inconsistent style. How else should one interpret the peculiar small figures sitting like cherubs on

the edge of a small balcony? Casa Vicens exemplifies how an unremark-
able house can become a small palace.

The attractiveness of the ornaments continues inside the house.
Here we also find a surprising mixture of styles which nevertheless creates the impression of stylistic purity – though only briefly.

On closer inspection of the details, the observer soon discovers
that this is not the case. Thus, the smoking room may come closest to
resembling a small Arabian cabinet. There is a water-pipe in the middle
of the room; lavishly upholstered chairs and divans are grouped around
it. Like the outer walls, those inside are covered with hand-painted tiles
with floral motifs, while the stalactite ceiling brings Moorish architecture to mind.

With the passage of time, the site underwent several changes. Both
the original railings and a small structure in the garden fell victim to a
road-widening scheme. The elaborate waterfall which Gaudí created in
the garden, for both its decorative and cooling effects, had to make way
for further development of the property, thus freeing up the area at the
back of the house, where Gaudí had installed a fire-resistant wall. This
enabled the architect Joan Baptista Serra de Martínez, commissioned in
1925 by the new owner Antoni Jover i Puig, to almost double the residential accommodation. In so doing, he almost exactly copied the existing
parts of Gaudí's building. As a result, to the modern eye, the house seems
like a single, unified structure.

ABOVE · The very realistic dwarf palm leaves on the gate and fence are made from wrought iron and mounted on a rolled steel support structure, with iron hibiscus flowers marking the joins.

RIGHT AND PAGE 76 · Balcony on the street side of the extension. The colourful tiles feature orange marigolds, like those Gaudí would have seen in the still untended piece of land.

FOLLOWING SPREAD · Gaudí's intricate metal fence echoes the leaves of the dwarf palm, so simultaneously linking and dividing the garden area. Hand-crafted spikes provide a finishing touch.

ABOVE AND RIGHT · The corner tower on the street side is an exact copy of the tower on the opposite side; only the putti are differently positioned.

PAGE 77 · A vase just like one to be found at Casa Battló was probably put in place by a resident.

CASA VICENS

PAGE 78 · The entrance to the
smoking room is hidden beneath
the corner tower on the garden side.

PAGE 79 · The newly-laid side
entrance which became necessary after the demolition of an
existing porch.

ABOVE · The dining room with its fireplace and elegant layout, which includes a number of paintings, 32 of which are work of Francesc Torrescassana i Sallarès and are integrated into the panelling. The polished upper wall surfaces are decorated with ivy leaf motifs.

ABOVE · The ceiling of a small room on the top floor was painted to look like a dome.

FOLLOWING SPREAD · The second-floor bedroom in a 1936 photograph. While the first floor was designed for guests and social gatherings, the private apartments were on the floor above.

BELOW · The original design and
layout of the drawing-room in the
over-decorated style of the period,
with many oriental references and
pieces of occasional furniture.

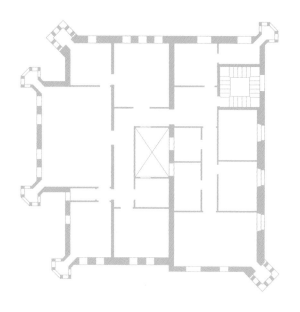

ABOVE · Daylight floods through a fanlight in the ceiling of the loggia next to the dining room.

RIGHT · A view of the smoking room. Above the hand-painted tiles on the lower walls with their rose motif, the upper section of the walls are clad with glazed tiling made from paper maché. The palm motifs on the ceiling are complemented by bunches of dates. Having been painted over in cream, the ceiling was stripped to reveal the original blue and gold colour scheme. The room would have been furnished with a sofa, stools and floor cushions, set around a small table with a hookah.

FOLLOWING SPREAD · Detail of the dining room ceiling. Cherry wood twigs cover the spaces between the beams, while shellfish mark where the ceiling meets the frieze. The passage leading to the loggia is home to a flock of birds painted by Josep Torrescassana.

EL CAPRICHO

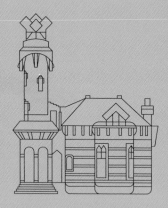

Barrio Sobrellano, Comillas

No one today will remember how this little house came to be called *El Capricho* – a mood, a caprice, perhaps also a whim. If it has anything to do with the playful impression created by the house, then it is deserving of its name. There it stands, as if it had dropped from the sky, from another world, and landed in the middle of a small green plot of land in Comillas near Santander. It is Gaudí's attempt to combine the Middle Ages, the golden age of Catalonia, with the grace and dignity of oriental residences. It looks cumbersome: a compact building with an evenly distributed tile pattern embedded in the brick walls. Even the tower, on its thick pillars, harks back to the Dark Ages. But then the slender, richly decorated tower rises cheekily like an inquisitive finger pointing into the air, and the little roof perched on top seems determined to defy all the laws of gravity.

PAGE 91 · The summerhouse's entrance portico grows upwards to become a watchtower reminiscent of a minaret of the Shah Mosque in Isfahan. Here Gaudí sets this colourful landmark on top of small round temple built of natural stone, whose four columns rise from their unadorned bases to floral capitals before moving upwards past architraves and arches to the base of the tower. This interplay between heaviness and lightness is a theme running through the entire building.

RIGHT · The watchtower walls are fully tiled while the platform displays vine tendrils. However, Gaudí wisely avoids an overabundance of biomorphic ornamentation by keeping the ironwork supporting the pinnacle plain and simple.

Actually, "El Capricho" would in fact have been an equally fitting nickname for the Casa Vicens. Both houses are colourful, resemble Moorish architecture, and were erected at about the same time. This may explain why, strictly speaking, these are twin buildings. The vaults and oriels – a constant source of surprise – and the variety of little towers on the Casa Vicens' roof makes for a much more capricious impression than the manor house built for Máximo Díaz de Quijano in Comillas, a small town near Santander. Here, too, the plot of land is not exactly large, yet the house stands, like an island, in the midst of its green surroundings. With this project Gaudí again achieved the impression of a Moorish-oriental style through the use of tiles with Spanish flower patterns. Instead of the tagetes employed for the Casa Vicens, he chose blossoms resembling sunflowers. The ornamentation of El Capricho is, however, much more subdued, less imaginative, and less colourful. The main body of the building comprises nine alternating rows of bricks and flowered tiles, creating a very calm rhythm.

However, "moody" (another meaning of "Capricho") is a fitting description for the minaret-like tower as it soars straight upwards; it is solely decorative with no function whatsoever for the actual house. "Mood" could also be used to characterise the peculiar little balconies protruding at the corners of the house, and for which Gaudí contrived an oversized trellis and "roof" made of thick, square iron bars. Although they appear to serve no purpose whatsoever, Gaudí used them to conceal a little surprise: he attached the counterweights for the sliding windows to two iron pipes in the trellis, so that when the windows are opened or closed the pipes begin to vibrate and produce strange sounds.

However, although the ornamentation of the façade seems somewhat staid by comparison with the colourful Casa Vicens – the architectonic structure of this, a bachelor's manor house, is freer and more playful than it is in the latter. As soon as we approach the entrance, we notice one of the "moods" of this house. The view of the door is almost completely blocked by four relatively thick pillars and their delicately designed capitals, which give way to three somewhat clumsy-looking rounded arches. The tower then rises up from this porticus. Despite all this masterfully executed whimsicality, however, Gaudí's talent as a pragmatist also came into its own. The roof – a part of the building to which the architect always devoted special attention – is relatively sober in Gaudí's terms, and above all surprisingly straight. He was making allowances for the local climate with its higher-than-average rainfall.

The design of the rooms differs considerably from that of the Casa Vicens. It is completely tailored to the needs of a wealthy bachelor. Whereas the dining room was the focus of the Casa Vicens – it was significantly larger than the other rooms – El Capricho is but a one-storey building and consists mainly of rooms for socialising purposes: several bedrooms and guest rooms, a lobby and above all a huge salon with a very high ceiling. This salon – a kind of winter-garden – forms the core of the house; the other rooms are grouped around it like additional extras. The lighting also differs from that of the Casa Vicens. The Casa Vicens has relatively few windows for its size, but the rooms seem all the more cosy and warm because of it. El Capricho, on the other hand, is filled with light. The walls of the main salon are to a large extent made up of huge windows separated from one another only by wooden posts, which in itself makes the room seem large, an impression which is further enhanced by its height. This feature does indeed transform the house into a whim of the architect. The salon is the only room which reaches up into the attic and even takes in part of the upper split level of the ground floor, the rest of which functions as the servants' lodgings – in other words, a room which is two storeys in height, but cuts across three floors.

Gaudí's approach to the design of this house was not at all typical of him. As a rule, he designed houses on the site where they were to be built, drawing additional inspiration from the location. Thus, his building projects "grew wild" in the course of their realisation, sometimes taking unpredictable turns. In the case of El Capricho he deviated from his customary approach. He engaged his friend Cristóbal Cascante i Colom to supervise the construction of the house, never visiting the building site itself, and he never met the client face to face. However, he must have had detailed descriptions of the site, as his design included numerous details which were meticulously adapted to the specific conditions of the area: the house stands on a slope, and part of the site therefore had to be built up to take this into account. Gaudí designed small "pillars" to serve as the supporting walls, which resemble the minaret-like turret of the house. Most importantly, however, the building was designed to encircle an existing hothouse, which occupied the opening in the U-shaped floorplan. It was here that Díaz kept the plants he had brought back from America and he wanted his new home to be built close to them. In the event, he did not live to see the completion of the house and in the end it was his sister who eventually moved into El Capricho.

Rumour has it that Gaudí later visited the property incognito, but in any case from then onwards he would only work in direct contact with the site and any pre-existing buildings.

LEFT · Despite the building's distinctly neo-Gothic character, Gaudí avoided pointed Gothic arches, preferring geometrically simpler forms, which can also be seen in the conservatory. The stained glass window with the bird perched on the organ keyboard adds a touch of humour.

ABOVE · This frieze runs along the edge of the wall panelling in the dining room.

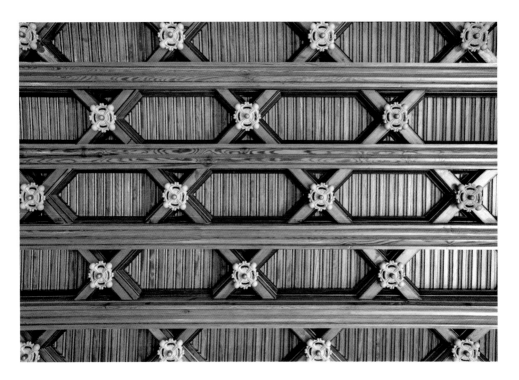

ABOVE · The ceiling of a space once used as a bedroom.

BELOW · Ground plan of the first floor. The portico with three short steps is set diagonally to the building's longitudinal axis.

RIGHT · The niche next to the games room also has a coffered ceiling. The residents liked to spend their evenings in this westward-facing room, since the bedroom faced east.

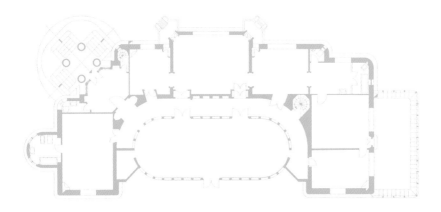

FINCA GÜELL

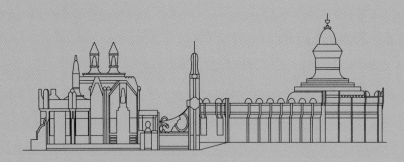

Avenida de Pedralbes, Barcelona

Gaudí adopted a rather chilling design for his third great architectural work, which is, in fact, a collection of several smaller buildings. There are virtually no outside windows, and the walls, a uniformly designed surface decorated with light, semi-circular ornamentation, could easily conceal a sultan's harem. The entrance could hardly be more austere. On the left, the corner of a small porter's lodge obstinately greets the visitor; on the right, the long, flat building with the sumptuous dome appears just as inaccessible. Anyone who is still undaunted and nevertheless wishes to enter then comes face to face with an iron dragon, which bars the way, forming the mighty iron gate. Although this imposing façade does not harbour a royal palace, but only the stables of a country estate, it gives some indication of the owner's wealth all the same.

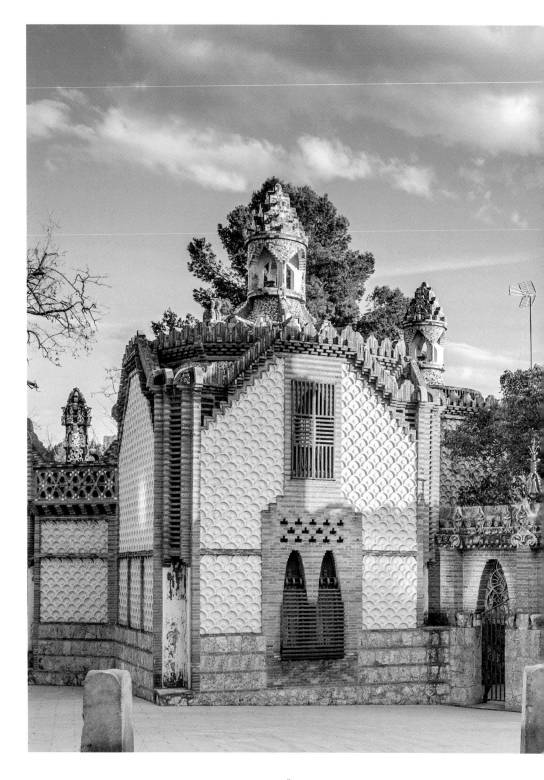

FINCA GÜELL

Even before Gaudí was commissioned by his friend and patron Eusebi
Güell to take on the ambitious project of erecting a palace-like residence in the centre of Barcelona, he had the opportunity to offer Güell
a few samples of his art. In 1883, Güell had acquired an estate outside
of what was then Barcelona, between Les Corts and Pedralbes. Gaudí
was to carry out some restoration work and construct a number of
additional buildings. In keeping with Güell's wishes – one of which
was to display his social standing – it was in particular the entrance
that was to be given a new design. The work on the estate was carried
out parallel to Gaudí's construction of the Güell Palace, but architectural worlds lie between the two projects. Although they were completed almost simultaneously, they mark two highly different phases
of Gaudí's creative work. The additional buildings for the estate are
clearly in line with the Mudejar style, which was also characteristic
of the Casa Vicens and El Capricho. When Gaudí designed the ornamental exterior of the last of these three buildings, his style was in
fact considerably purer than for the other two – if one can speak of
stylistic purity at all in Gaudí's architecture. The light, semi-circular
patterns with which he decorated the façades are one example. Gaudí
used an abstract motif instead of the indigenous tagetes or sunflower
patterns used in his earlier works. The little turret, which rises above
the flattened dome of the riding school, is much more reserved and
refined in design than the fanciful turret of El Capricho. Gaudí's use
of a uniform pattern for the façade was his way of showing that, as far
as he was concerned, the project was based on a single, coherent plan,
although it consisted of such diverse buildings as stables, riding hall
and a porter's lodge.

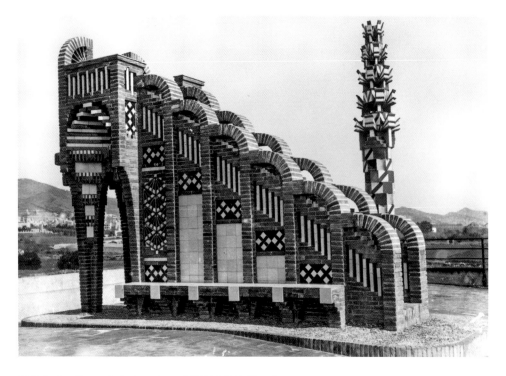

ABOVE · Gaudí not only designed the gatehouse to Güell's estate, but also fountains, a cart shelter and two vantage points, one of them on the roof of the house.

RIGHT ABOVE · First-floor ground plan of Finca Güell's two buildings, consisting of three structures, the gatehouse, stables and riding school.

The Pavilions bear an unmistakable resemblance to both of the Moorish works that preceded them, and yet Gaudí designed something entirely new with these three small buildings. The most fascinating aspect of them is above all the design of the interior. The porter's lodge, for example, is a single-storey octagon, but with the compactness of a cube, topped by a flattened dome – an innovation in Gaudí's formal idiom. The cupola is even repeated in the square towers adjoining the octagon. The stables are housed in a long, flat building with the same ornamentation on the façade as that used in the porter's lodge: this is the only feature indicating that these two structures belong together. The adjoining riding hall, which served as a riding school, is hardly distinguishable from the stables. Only a cupola with a small tower showing Moorish inspiration

BELOW · The large main gate was built by the locksmiths Vallet i Piquer in 1885. It shows Ladon, the mythological dragon that guarded the golden apples in the Garden of the Hesperides. The dragon's claws move when the gate is opened.

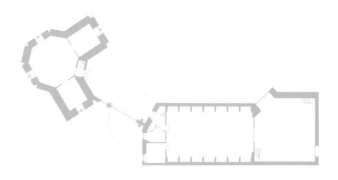

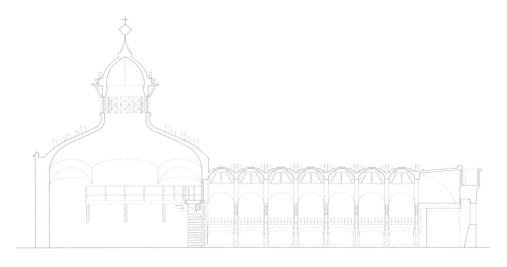

PREVIOUS SPREAD · Panels of cement, in those days a very modern building material, line the walls of the building.

BELOW · The light-filled riding hall featuring white painted arches was used by the university's architecture institute for several years.

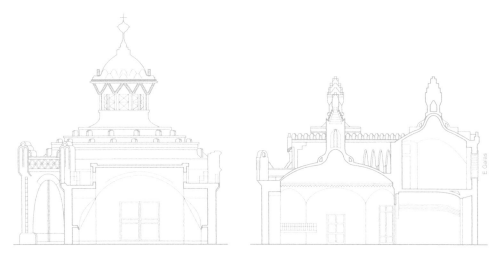

LEFT ABOVE AND ABOVE ·
Cross sections of the riding
school and gatehouse.

alludes to its special function. The turrets on the riding hall and on the porter's lodge create a kind of formal parenthesis which fuses the highly diverse buildings into a whole.

The interior design of the stables is particularly noteworthy. Connoisseurs of Gaudí's late works will be quick to notice this when visiting the estate, and may be led to think that they can detect the early signs of Gaudí's later preoccupation with high, vaulted arches. The stables are spanned by a series of thick, arching walls in bright white plaster. As a result, they look amazingly expansive, wide and light. However, these arches do not take an extreme, parabolic form. They do not so much anticipate Gaudí's later carrying arches as hark back to the factory hall in Mataró. Nevertheless, the design is bold and modern in effect. Above all, it is surprisingly down-to-earth compared with the rich decor of the outside walls.

However, the gate that runs between the porter's lodge and the stables is probably more impressive than the stables themselves. It is an eminent example of Gaudí's talent for ironwork. It is also one of the first major examples of the art nouveau elements in his work. Moreover, it is proof of Gaudí's great skills as a designer and structural engineer. It is 15 feet wide and yet consists of only a single piece; in other words, it is hinged on only one side. Gaudí thus had to use a very tall hinge pole – more than 30 feet high. If Gaudí had designed the gate symmetrically – as was commonly the case – it would have looked like the gate to a prison. But instead he set the top of the iron gate at a little more than half of the 30-foot height, lending it a fanciful elegance. The lower half of the gate consists of a pattern made of little square metal plates, which looks translucent. Above it, in a multitude of sweeping lines, rises a huge dragon with terrifying gaping jaws; this gave the gate its name and is also an early example of the symbolism in Gaudí's work: the dragon watches over the garden, and fanciful though it may seem, owing to the myriads of art nouveau twirls, it nevertheless fulfils its function very effectively: whenever anyone tries to open the gate, the dragon's claw rises up with its strong iron talons.

These are the major works that Gaudí designed for the Güell estate. Several of the plans for the numerous minor projects – which included redesigning the old Güell residence and a perimeter wall for the cemetery – were eventually withdrawn. They are only of secondary importance and come nowhere close to matching the quality of the dragon gate, which ranks as a masterpiece of Catalonian ironwork to the present day.

GÜELL PALACE

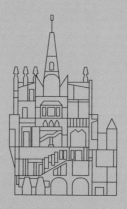

Calle Nou de la Rambla, Barcelona

No matter where one stands in the Calle Nou de la Rambla, it is difficult to get a full view of the palace Gaudí built for his friend Eusebi Güell. Not because of its size: the site is only 54 x 66 feet. The most one would normally build on a piece of land this size is a respectable middle-class home. However, the street is so narrow that it is impossible to step back far enough to have a good view of the entire palace (which, incidentally, is not in the best of neighbourhoods). All one can see from one of the houses across the road is a plain front made of large stone blocks. One sees little of the lavishly decorated façade on the lower floors, but cannot help noticing onthe palace roof the bizarre turrets which adorned all the chimneys subsequently designed by Gaudí. This is a palace with a fairy-tale garden on the roof.

PAGE 119 · The austerity of the limestone façade is relieved by the protruding oriels. The limestone came from Güell's own quarry in Garraf. Below on the right is the staff entrance.

LEFT · A vertical arrangement of loggias and balconies, shaded by wooden slats, contrasts with the simplicity of the building's rear façade which overlooks the courtyard.

When Gaudí became Eusebi Güell's favourite architect in the mid-1880s, he had very few works to his name. The Casa Vicens was still in progress, and El Capricho was about to be completed. The businessman's appreciation for Gaudí's work was actually based on the samples he had seen at the Paris World's Fair. There were many times in Gaudí's life when his patrons demonstrated their confidence in his work, even though his style had yet to mature and prove itself. Güell sensed the extent of Gaudí's talent, but he was surely also attracted to Gaudí because of the young architect's social commitment to the working classes and his Catalonian convictions. Gaudí, for his part, was fascinated by Güell's rare combination of nobility, financial power and commitment to the cause of the lower classes. When he designed a coat of arms for Güell, he added the words: "Yesterday a shepherd, today a man of nobility", to put Güell's career in a nutshell – a man who had grown up in humble circumstances, but later returned from a stay in America with a sizeable fortune to his name. When he commissioned Gaudí to build a palace in the middle of Barcelona, money was no longer an object. At one point, an employee in charge of managing Güell's finances once called the art patron's attention to the enormous rise in the project's costs. "I fill Don Eusebio's pockets," he is said to have lamented, "and Gaudí then empties them." This criticism, however, fell on deaf ears.

In return, of course, Güell acquired something of value which could not be measured in money. Yet the conditions were anything but favourable. The Comte de l'Assalt (known today as Calle Nou de la Rambla) where the palace was to be erected is a narrow street, and the construction site was by no means large: 54 x 66 feet is not much space for an average palace, not even for an urban palace. Gaudí drafted no fewer than

18 plans for the façade alone. He finally decided on a design which was a surprisingly reserved, austere version of his previous works. The front of the house, which directly joins the adjacent building, is characterised by right angles, and the main decoration is the slightly protruding balcony on the first floor, which extends to the second floor only at the ends. Gaudí almost completely dispensed with sculptural ornamentation; only between the two large entrances did he agree to mount a splendid Catalan coat of arms – a clear allusion to his patron's political leanings (as well as his own). Because of this austere façade with its clear lines, covered with grey polished marble plates, the palace looks larger than it actually is. It resembles somewhat the urban palaces in Renaissance Venice; perhaps this was Gaudí's way of erecting a monument to Güell's mother, who came from Italy – albeit not from the nobility.

This historicising façade is, however, broken up by an extremely anachronistic element. Two enormous gates made of iron lattice rise before the visitor's eyes, who in the narrow street cannot step back far enough to appreciate its full effect (this is why these gates are frequently photographed from one side, usually with a wide-angle lens, which makes it seem as if they are leaning backwards). These gates became quite an attraction because they were the first of their kind in Barcelona and therefore bound to meet with scepticism and rejection. Eventually, such gates became quite commonplace. They are only one example of the way Gaudí set architectural trends. The gates have a peculiar arch shape, which is neither pointed and Gothic nor rounded and Arabic, a type of arch that had such a strong influence on Gaudí's first works. This was the first time that Gaudí employed the parabolic arch design which would reappear in all of his subsequent works and which he would later

develop into a carrying element of his buildings. (This element made it possible for him to do without the flying buttresses and arches he disliked so much in Gothic architecture.) The parabolic forms appear once more in the interior of the building, where Gaudí even experimented with the Gothic tradition. In the lobby on the main floor of the palace, the light that falls through the windows is subdued by three huge parabolic arches formed by grey, smoothly polished stone pillars. The towering arches create the impression of a Gothic window; but the windows which Gaudí employed in Güell's palace are rectangular – in other words, they serve as a counterpoint to the lines of the arches. In this lobby Gaudí again broke with predominant forms of architecture – a break which was initiated by the round archway he had used on the outside façade.

The top third of each arch is lavishly decorated by interwoven iron bars, in which one can see the owner's initials; they are framed by a twisting line which strongly resembles a horse-whip. This was Gaudí's reference to the actual function of these gates, which at the same time justified their completely disproportionate size: they were designed to enable guests to ride through this entranceway in their carriages. In the lobby, he designed a gently sloping ramp for the horses, leading down to the sub-level, i.e. the stables. Like the gate design, this was also an innovation in Barcelona's architecture. Gaudí's real debut as an architect in this city – the Casa Vicens was located more on the outskirts, in the Gràcia district – was breathtaking. Elaborate pieces of decorative art also play a key role inside the building. For one thing, there are lavish decorations on the pillars, of which there are a considerable number: from the thick, supporting, mushroom-shaped pillars in the basement all the way to the elegant, expensive, smoothly polished grey pillars made of

LEFT · The conical spire of the central turret culminates in a stylised sun, above which is a small dragon-shaped weathervane, crowned by a cross emphasising the Christian religion.

RIGHT · Gaudí is reputed to have sketched 18 variations for the street side of the building, two of which he presented to the client, who decided on the version with the two large arches above the entrance.

BELOW · In the carefully-observed hierarchical structure of the rear façade, the second floor is glorified by the line of yellow ceramic tiles.

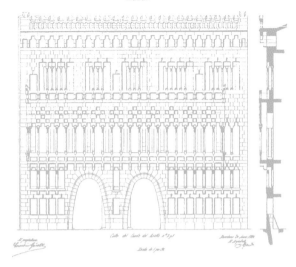

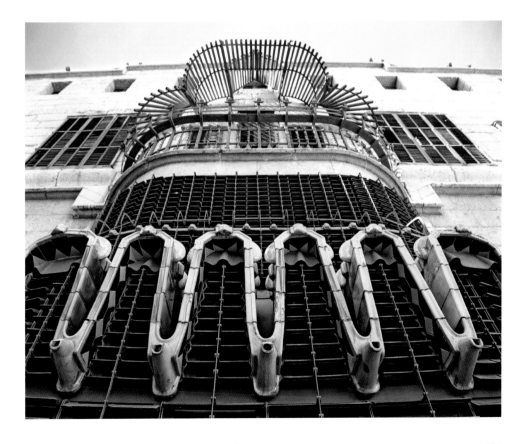

GÜELL PALACE

GÜELL PALACE

PREVIOUS SPREAD · There appears to have been no specific plan behind the huge variety of decorative elements used.

LEFT · Three chimneys on the front side of the building.

snake-eye stone excavated from a quarry in the Pyrenees. There are a total of 127 pillars in the palace, which generally created the impression of overwhelming size – an optical illusion for which Gaudí was in all likelihood deliberately striving. Indeed, he was quite willing to allow for distorted proportions in order to achieve this. The entrance portals are out of all proportion to the surface area of the façade as a whole. Yet, when one stands before them, one cannot help but have the feeling that one is viewing a palace of immeasurable size. One has a similar impression when climbing the steps to the first main floor (the building has six floors in all). A hall spanning three floors forms the centre of the building. It replaces, as it were, the normal inner courtyard, but at the same time creates the impression that one is standing in a huge baroque church. This room is covered by a cupola in which Gaudí put numerous round holes. Thus, it looks as if starlight was falling directly into the building. As grandiose as this middle room may seem, however, it only has a surface of 27 square feet, and a height of 52 feet. It is this height that makes the hall look so overwhelming. And it is here that social life takes place. Gaudí designed an organ for the music-lover Güell, placing the pipes in the upper gallery. The music thus seems to cascade down over the listeners from on high. An altar rounds out the design of this unique room, which was originally intended to play only a marginal role. However, in the course of the planning the architect and owner alike became so enthusiastic with regard to the room that it eventually became the heart and soul of the building. It seems as if the other rooms of the house, of which there are no small number, were built around it: it is a kind of hyper-dimensional pillar which "bears" the rest of the building.

RIGHT · A mezzanine was reserved for Güell's office. The way up from the first floor to the private apartments led diagonally through an anteroom which formed part of the business premises.

FOLLOWING SPREAD · The coffered ceiling in the drawing-room. Stained glass medallions set in the windows depict characters from Shakespeare's plays.

The other rooms are, of course, not merely of secondary importance. Gaudí took great care in designing the ceilings, which are lavishly decorated with wooden ornamentation, eucalyptus and cypress panels, complemented (and at the same time supported) by richly decorated iron components; there are no stable elements bearing the weight of the ceiling. In addition to the architectural design of the building itself, the furniture designed by Gaudí is particularly noteworthy because it reflects his very own version of art nouveau. There are the typical fanciful forms, yet they are accompanied by surprisingly plain forms. The mirror on the dressing table on the upper floor looks like a collage of traditional rectangular mirrors with elegant twirls of art nouveau at its base, thus combining two totally different styles of mirror. The two wooden elements on which it rests – or seems to be balanced, actually – are no less original. They are little pillars; and the feet look like oddly bent, surreal three-dimensional figures. A curved iron bar connects these pillars and, once again, Gaudí was thinking in practical terms: they were a useful support "when tying one's shoelaces". In the case of later buildings, the workers were often very sceptical about Gaudí's designs and asked how they were supposed to stay standing. The same question inevitably comes to mind when one views the dressing table. It seems as if the mirror is about to fall down at any moment.

The building's biggest surprise, however, awaits visitors on the roof, with its colourful forest of ceramic-tiled chimneys and ventilation shafts and its central turret. The roof was always an important element for Gaudí, and he gave his fertile imagination free rein in designing it. And it never bothered him that the forms, many of which are quite bizarre, could usually not be seen from the street. The roof is topped by

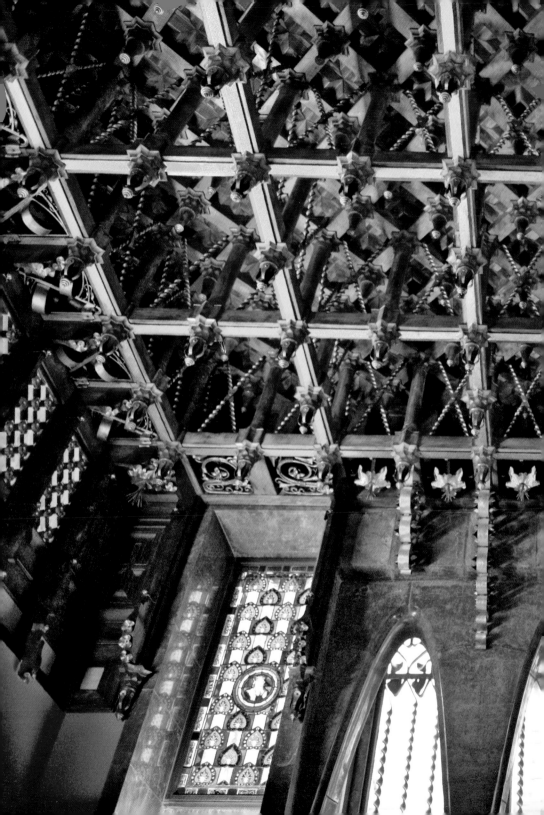

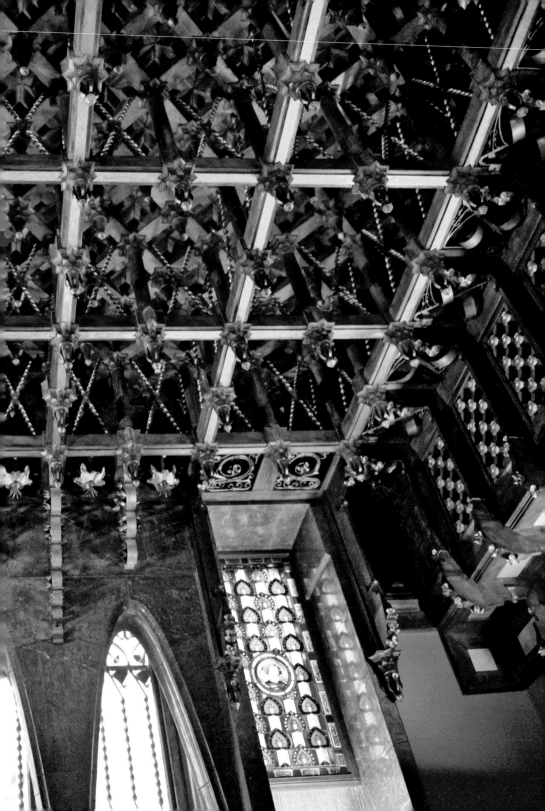

ABOVE · On the floor where the private apartments were situated, between the bathroom and the bedrooms was a *Sala de Confiança*, an intimate space in which to meet trusted friends and acquaintances.

Above the open fireplace is a picture of St Elizabeth, the work of the well-known poster artist, Alexandre de Riquer i Ynglada. The room, like all the others on this floor, has natural stone-tiled flooring.

RIGHT · View down into the hall from the private apartments, including the open door to the private altar.

PREVIOUS SPREAD · View from the main hall to the *Sala de passos perduts* – hall of lost steps –, through which, after many twists and turns, visitors finally reached the centre of the building.

ABOVE · A small mezzanine, fitted in between the main floor and the private apartments, provides space for a musicians' gallery. On the hall side, the space is enclosed by a delicately-carved, Moorish-style, wooden screen with ivory inlays.

RIGHT · This picture shows how the musicians' gallery fitted into the main hall. The musicians, together with the organ on the upper floor and singers in front-of-house, created an acoustic system capable of producing a complete work of musical art. This cultural aspiration was complemented by an extensive program of visual art, for which the painter Aleix Clapés i Puig was commissioned.

No more than a room divider
made of perforated wood sepa-
rates the smoking room, with its
settee in the bay window, from
the neighbouring family parlour.

a small cupola which rises above the hall in the centre and tapers off into a pointed tower, lending the building a peculiarly religious air. Yet the tower clashes completely with the rest of the building – even in its colour; it is simply stuck on the top. It is surrounded by 18 surrealistic "sculptures" which remind one of the legs of the dressing table. They are early examples of the little turrets Gaudí was later to sublimate in the form of the mitre-like spires of the Sagrada Familia: small, often twisted, formations with additional ornamental points and corners, which look like sheer playfulness and yet, as so often in Gaudí's works, serve highly practical purposes – they are both chimney decorations and ventilation ducts. Gaudí detracted from the ordinary function of these elements by adding the lavish ornamentation of colourful tiles.

This palace immediately wrested Gaudí from anonymity. During the construction work (from 1886 to 1889, an amazingly short time) numerous reports appeared in the press (even in American newspapers) which at first only named the owner of the house, but they soon turned their attention to the young architect as well, who had set out so unabashedly on an entirely new architectural path.

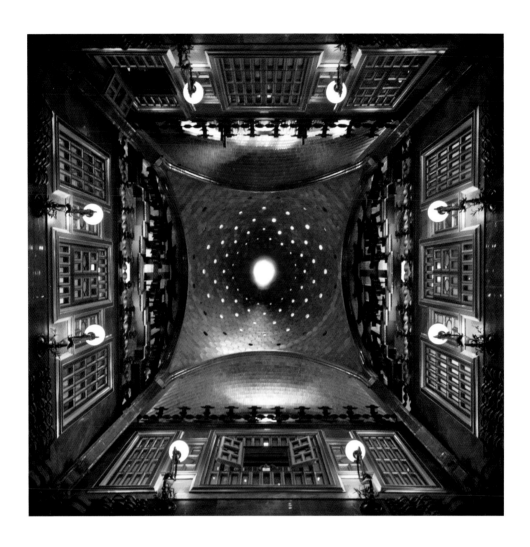

ABOVE · View from below of the dome above the main hall. The gallery around which the bedrooms are arranged overlooks the main hall through windows with gilded frames. The transom windows are so constructed that visitors viewing from below cannot see through them. However, the gilding, combined with natural daylight, creates a fascinating kind of luminosity, although the hall itself remains in darkness.

RIGHT · Eusebi Güell commissioned the Basque organ builder, Aquilino Amezua y Jáuregui, to build the organ for his townhouse. The keyboard was placed on the main floor while the pipes were set high above, surrounding the cupola. When that organ had to be replaced, some of its original parts were put into use to enable the organist to sit on the same level as instrument.

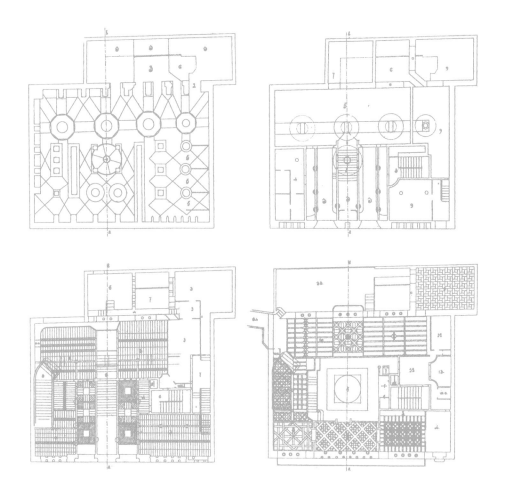

ABOVE · Ground plan of the building.

RIGHT · Stained glass window in the private apartments.

FOLLOWING SPREAD · View from the mezzanine into the main room of the business premises. Like the neighboring anteroom, it had a single column standing in the middle.

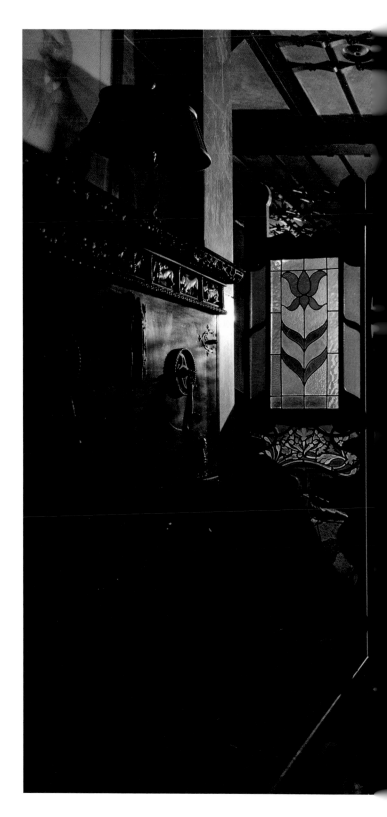

ABOVE · The lavishly-decorated walnut fireplace in the dining room was the work of the cabinetmaker Camil Oliveras i Gensana.

RIGHT · The parlour, the anteroom and the terrace all provided direct access to Eusebi Güell's father's house.

FOLLOWING SPREAD · An historical photo of the main hall.

ABOVE · The identical candelabra on either side of the main entrance to the hall means that looking through the doorway is like looking in a mirror.

RIGHT · View of the *hall of lost steps* from the large main hall. The parabolic shape of the arches set in the wall give a foretaste of what is to come.

FOLLOWING SPREAD · Enormous brick columns dominate the basement. At one time the stables were here and could be reached via a spiral ramp.

BISHOP'S PALACE

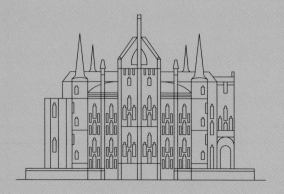

Plaza de Eduardo Castro, Astorga

If there is a building of Gaudí's to which the term neo-Gothic applies, then it must surely be the Bishop's Palace in Astorga near León. The old palace had been destroyed by fire and in 1887 Bishop Joan Baptista Grau i Vallespinós commissioned Gaudí to design a new palace. Grau, like Gaudí, came from Reus. Before being ordained bishop, he had been the vicar-general for the Archdiocese of Tarragona. The contract was not exactly timely as far as Gaudí was concerned; he was in the middle of drawing up plans for the Sagrada Familia, and work on the Güell Palace was still underway.

BISHOP'S PALACE

PAGE 165 · View of the Episcopal Palace from the street with the main entrance and the proposed office space on the right.

PREVIOUS SPREAD · Gaudí designed three angel figures that he wanted to install on the roof. This did not happen after he withdrew

from the project. Nevertheless, they were constructed and now stand in the garden: they present the crosier, the bishop's mitre and the cross.

LEFT · An historical view of the protruding apse of the chapel, which in turn is surrounded by three smaller apses.

FOLLOWING SPREAD · Vaults in the crypt directly under the chapel. However enclosed the building may appear, the interior spaces are full of light.

Gaudí did not make a simple project of the task. He requested that he be given exact plans of the site and photographs of the surroundings: it was above all the latter that played an important part in his design of the exterior of the building. The bishop was delighted with the plans; the Real Academia de Bellas Artes de San Fernando in Madrid, whose approval was necessary before work could go ahead, was somewhat more reserved. This was just a foretaste of the problematic situation Gaudí was to experience during construction work until building activities were broken off prematurely in 1893. As long as his patron, the bishop, was still alive, Gaudí managed to put his ideas into practice, after he had twice revised plans to suit the wishes of the Academy. Quite out of keeping with his later custom, Gaudí drafted precisely drawn plans for the building, apparently in part because he wanted to pre-empt the objections he anticipated.

Gaudí oriented himself above all towards the neo-Gothicism propagated by Viollet-le-Duc, which was in line with the character and function of the building. This theorist had recommended that an intensive study of old Gothic buildings should precede any new architecture, but had advised strictly against simply copying such forms.

Gaudí perfected this undertaking. He approximated his work so closely to his historical models that he even used French Gothic capitals for the columns on the main floor: the eight-pronged, star-shaped abacuses are direct imitations of the Sainte-Chapelle in Paris. The sense of Gothicism surrounding the building is otherwise not pronounced. The round towers remind one more of a castle than a sacred building. Although the starkly protruding entrance contains monumental arches, they have been flattened out so that they do not thrust upwards but seem

RIGHT · Floor plan of the ground floor. All the spaces are of full height and are positioned around a central area.

FAR RIGHT · Pillars and vaults in the lower hall. The rib vaulting is enhanced by the use of glazed bricks.

rather to bow forward. The apexes of the windows are also only mildly pointed. It is only the dining room on the first floor that has predominantly Gothic traits. Nevertheless, some critics have described this building as the best example of Spanish neo-Gothic architecture.

Gaudí used white granite for the outer façade. This material was adopted because of the fascination it exerted on the eye, but it also had a spiritual function for Gaudí: the Bishop's Palace was supposed to accord optically with the white of the bishop's robes. This white façade was to climax gloriously in the equally white roof, but things never got that far. Bishop Grau died before building work was completed, and from the very beginning the administration of the diocese had not held Gaudí's plans in particularly high esteem. Following the bishop's death, it tried to intervene in the work, whereupon Gaudí abandoned the project. It is said that he even intended to burn the plans, although he did not. It was his wish that the building remain unfinished; he swore himself never to set foot in Astorga again, not even to cross over it in a balloon.

It was some time before the building was completed. The architects who took up the work deviated from his plans so that part of the building collapsed. It was not ready for habitation until 1961.

LEFT · The office was never used for what it was intended, as the palace as a whole never became the Bishop's residence. The stained-glass windows were designed Daniel Zuloaga Boneta.

ABOVE · The so-called dining room on the second floor of the Episcopal Palace in Astorga. The door leads on to a small balcony above the entrance.

FOLLOWING SPREAD · The chapel is lavishly decorated. It was a collaborative effort shared by several artists, including the sculptor, Enrique Marín e Higuero, and the painter, Fernando de Villodas.

COLEGIO TERESIANO

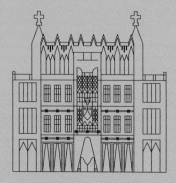

Calle de Ganduxer, Barcelona

Basking in the rays of sun from the south and against the background of a blue sky, the building radiantly shines forth in all its splendour. The large coat of arms of the order housed here – the Order of St Teresa of Ávila – stands out colourfully. But the impression is deceptive. Frugality and austerity were the highest commandments of the order, and Gaudí, too, had to abide by them. Thus, the balcony, which rises like a tower above the entrance, is nearly the only decoration in what is, by Gaudí's standards, an ascetic structure. Only the parapet, which runs in a zig-zag pattern along the edge of the roof, is pure pomp. But it is also representative of the style of the building as a whole, which was devoted completely to the saint who gave the order its name, St Teresa, who was guided by mediaeval philosophy, the pinnacle of the Gothic style. Gaudí followed suit in his own manner.

Even as a student, Gaudí had concentrated on ecclesiastic building projects, although consistently sticking to ideas far less eclectic than those he applied to secular designs. Many of these earlier works tended to be small; here he created an altar, there he designed a reliquary shrine, but none of these received much critical attention. After an extremely pious upbringing, in his student days other things became more important to him, but he refused to be much influenced by the widespread wave of anti-clericalism that arose in 1872. Instead, on completing his studies, he met several people whose friendship he came to treasure and who guided him towards a spiritual approach to religion. In the course of his life, Gaudí was increasingly drawn to a life of asceticism, which also found expression architecturally in the school and headquarters of the Order of St Teresa (of Ávila). As for the costs, Gaudí had been accustomed to having abundant resources at his disposal for the design of his first works; even in the Casa Vicens project, where the owner had not had limitless means available, money had been no object. When he tackled the project for the convent, he was still spending money left and right for the Güell Palace. The Colegio Teresiano was another matter altogether, as the order had made frugality its prime commandment. The budget allocated for Gaudí's work was not lavish. The fact that he kept to this budget shows the extent to which he always adjusted his building plans to the modalities at hand – be it to the local conditions of the building site or the message the structure was to convey (such as the historical past of Catalonia, which he incorporated into the design of Bellesguard). Gaudí was nevertheless not spared several critical remarks made by Father Enric d'Ossó i Cervelló, the founder of the order. When the latter admonished him because of the expense, Gaudí revealed his obstinate

temperament: "To each his own, Father Enric," he is supposed to have replied. "I build houses, you read masses and say prayers."

The order was still very young, having only been founded in 1876. The target of criticism was the mounting bills for bricks, and not without justification. Gaudí's work on the Colegio Teresiano was not only subject to tight constraints in terms of the available budget; the order's ideal of poverty by definition also incorporated the ideals of austerity, sobriety and frugality in every respect. Gaudí on the whole abided by this rule, even though it must have been difficult for him to do so. Nor was he at liberty to pursue any design he wished. The first floor of the order's building was already standing; in other words, as in the case of the Sagrada Familia, Gaudí had to proceed from a design that was not his own, only in this case it was much more confining. The entire shape of the floorplan of the house had been prescribed: a strictly rectangular, drawn-out building. The floors constructed above it, however, bear Gaudí's unmistakable mark. The floorplan divides the building lengthwise into three narrow sections which run parallel to each other. The basement of the middle section includes a long, narrow corridor; just above this, on the ground floor, rectangular inner courtyards allow the light to shine in the rooms on the inside. These inner courtyards are continued on the upper floors. Normally, such a construction on the inside of a building would have required two carrying walls along the length of it – which in fact exist on the ground floor. However, Gaudí altered the supporting structure on the remaining floors. Instead of the carrying walls he employed long corridors consisting of a single row of symmetrical, identical parabolic arches. In so doing, Gaudí accomplished several things at once: first of all, he eliminated the need for a carrying structure based on a long, uninteresting-looking wall; this way, he introduced some variety into the rigid lines of the building, which was already austere enough as it was. Secondly, he created generous corridors which almost form a kind of cloister, owing to the series of parallel arches. These arches are white-washed, with numerous windows spaced between them, opening onto the inner courtyard. As a result, the corridor is brightly, but indirectly, lit; the light is evenly distributed, lending the hall a quiet, contemplative atmosphere. At the same time, the all-pervading arch design alludes to the Gothic style, and thus, to a period which was also a focal point for the Carmelite order founded by St Theresa. In fact, Gaudí made this arch design the pivotal stylistic element of the building. Pointed arches dominate the overall appearance. The outer façade along the entire upper floor is marked by a row of pointed arch designs of various heights. The protruding covered balcony at the entrance, which breaks up the strict rectangular line of the floorplan, contains pointed arch windows, and the windows of the other floors resemble pointed arches as well. However, Gaudí also introduced a counterbalance to this underlying Gothic element: the window shutters, which are usually closed, repeat the rectangular form of the floorplan. The balcony over the entrance is also primarily characterised by rectangular designs.

Gaudí accomplished all this with simple and above all inexpensive materials. Large blocks of undressed stone alternate with broad sections of brick wall. Nevertheless, Ossó's criticism was justified. Gaudí permitted himself a certain amount of luxury in a few places, even if only with this quite inexpensive material. For example, along the top floor he added a row of brick parapets, again drawing on the underlying Gothic style, as a decorative finish to the façade. Thus, a delicate row of zig-zags rises up

against the horizon. His use of false brick arches in the large hall spaces was another luxury. They have no carrying function, but lend the halls a ceremonial and somewhat old-fashioned touch. Without these added touches the building might have been more in keeping with the basic principles of the order, but the halls would have been too bare. Gaudí combined whitewashed sections of wall with brick walls and in this way created a synthesis of the ascetic and of rustic, simple homeliness. From the strict standpoint of the order, the only thing for which he could be taken to task would be the spiralled, inward-turning brick pillars, which are a little reminiscent of the spiralling chimneys on the roof of the Güell Palace (which later also reappear as the bosses on the bell towers of the Sagrada Familia). This was the only playful excursion into the realm of the purely ornamental that Gaudí allowed himself.

On the other hand, he kept entirely to the main principle of the order. Gaudí's work on the convent marks the beginning of his steadily growing preoccupation with symbolic references. For example, he topped the pointed parapets on the roof with small mortarboards, a sign of his reverence for St Teresa, the scholar. However, they were soon removed (in 1936). The order's coat of arms appears six times, the most lavish instance being on the balcony in the middle of the main façade. St Teresa's initials also appear six times in the wrought-iron grating. A band of two bricklayers runs between the upper floors in the middle of the undressed stone front to the outer façade, and the initials of the name Jesus are burnt into the ceramic plates. These initials appear a total of 127 times in ceramic, and another 35 times on wrought-iron gratings. One can count many more. Such references could be interpreted as pure playfulness, but Gaudí integrated such allusions discreetly. One

ABOVE · Corridor on the second floor. The highly effective use of whitewash is one the artistic characteristics of the Mudejar style.

RIGHT · Here, Gaudí broke completely away from the neo-baroque room construction of the Episcopal Palace in Astorga and developed a structure based on interconnecting spaces and skilful use of light.

LEFT AND FOLLOWING SPREAD ·
Natural light has been cleverly used
in these corridors surrounding the
interior courtyard. The whitewashed
walls create a luminous effect.

has to look very closely in order to find them. In this way, the building becomes a little mystery; the "revelation" is concealed. It is necessary to become deeply engrossed in exploring the secrets of the building, which in a sense make it an embodiment of the order's saint: the house of the mystic is itself a small mystery. It is questionable whether all of its contemporaries recognised it for what it was. Otherwise, people would not have been so quick to remove one of its most genuinely symbolic elements, namely, the mortarboards (which were probably taken merely as a quirk of the architect, a man already known for his bizarre sense of architectonic humour).

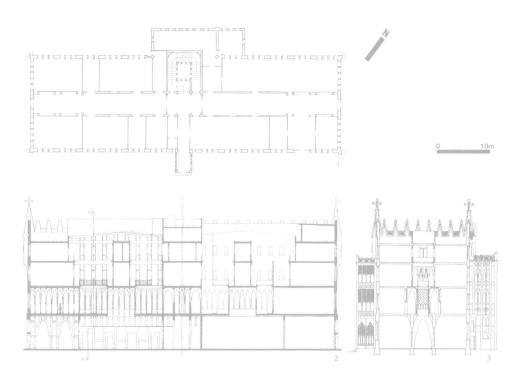

0 10m

LEFT · Contemporary photo of a classroom. The plant was probably placed there just for the photograph to give the somewhat austere room a little less gloomy.

ABOVE · Ground plan and sectional views.

1891—1894

CASA
BOTINES

Plaza de San Marcelo, León

As Gaudí had meanwhile established contacts with a wealth of people, the number of works he was contracted to do increased. While still undertaking the last work on the Bishop's Palace in Astorga (difficulties were already looming on the horizon with the administration of the diocese) he was commissioned to construct a further building in León. Two Gaudí buildings in such a small town – what opulence! At the end of the 19th century León had a mere 16,000 inhabitants and was not exactly distinguished by architectonic highlights. A few larger buildings from the past at least gave the face of the town some substance: a cathedral built between the 13th and 15th centuries, the large monastery of San Marcos and a somewhat sober Renaissance palace.

PAGE 199 · View of one the roofs of the building. Gaudí had the original idea of installing fanlights to provide lighting for the top floor.

LEFT · One of the corner turrets. During construction, there were critics who doubted whether Gaudí's building was sufficiently stable. However, to this day, there has been no indication of structural weakness.

FOLLOWING SPREAD · Completely different from what the exterior of the building might suggest, the interior rooms are bright and spacious.

Gaudí's work was not carried out under a particularly lucky star. His design for the foundations was not in keeping with the usual style of building in the town; people bemoaned the absence of pillars, and when Gaudí constructed the bases for the turrets on the first floor, turrets which he had intended as decoration for the sides of the building, there was a general fear that the Casa Botines (named after the founder of the company Joan Horns i Botinàs) would collapse. The building stood firm despite all the forebodings and today still shows no signs of age.

After the founder's death, firstly his brother-in-law and a colleague from the company took charge and were later joined by another colleague. Finally, the firm began trading as Fernández and Andrés, which is why the building is also known as Casa Fernández y Andrés. Among the textile company's suppliers was a business owned by Eusebi Güell, who recommended Gaudí to them as a suitable architect, especially as the ambitious young designer was often in the vicinity working on the Episcopal Palace.

Simón Fernández and Mariano Andrés González Luna purchased a plot of land centrally situated on León's market square. There, they wanted to erect a building combining storage space and offices in the basement and on the ground floor; two first-class apartments for the two owners on the first floor; and several rental apartments on the second and attic floors. Gaudí stuck strictly to the specifications, creating an infrastructure to suit the needs of the assorted users of the building, including doorways on three sides of the freestanding structure, thus avoiding friction between the various parties.

In order to provide flexible usage of space, Gaudí largely avoided load-bearing walls. The iron pillars supporting the ceilings did not adhere to the usual grid pattern, instead following the obliquely angled

CASA BOTINES

RIGHT ABOVE · View of the central part of the façade with the entrance, above which there is a large statue of St George killing the dragon.

RIGHT BELOW · Ground plan of the first floor.

floorplan. This is not immediately apparent, as the retaining walls of both stairwells keep to the asymmetric lines of the building. Even from outside, where the massive rusticated stone walls predominate, its uneven shape is barely noticeable.

The building's vast, awe-inspiring dimensions suggest a castle rather than an apartment building. This is partly due to the nature of the neighbourhood. Right next door to Casa Botines was the Palacio de los Guzmanes. To some degree Gaudí took this into consideration, insofar as he completed his building with rounded oriel side windows, which, in common with the towers, soar upward to a point, lending added interest to the somewhat austere roof. It stands on the central square in León, the Plaza de San Marcelo, like some large mass of stone. In contrast to the hefty underlying form, Gaudí – in keeping with his style at the time – made use of neo-Gothic elements, but only sparingly. The windows are often divided into three parts, which makes them seem broad, and are rounded at the top. Only the oriels that rise out of the edge of the roof have a spiky Gothic shape. The building clearly belongs in the trio of Gaudí's buildings inspired by Gothic architecture, and, together with the Bishop's Palace in Astorga and the Colegio Teresiano, can be viewed as constituting a distinctive series in Gaudí's opus. Today, it still towers above the rest of the town, and the inhabitants have obviously grown accustomed to it. Gaudí mounted a statue of St George the Dragon-slayer above the main entrance. Plans in 1950 to remove this statue met with a general wave of protest. The sculpture stayed where it was. Nowadays, one does not go about disfiguring works of the famous Catalonian architect without thinking twice.

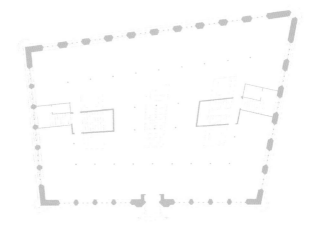

1897—1900

BODEGAS GÜELL

Garraf, Sitges

The bodegas (wine cellars) which Gaudí built for his patron Eusebi Güell in Garraf near Sitges are usually not mentioned in the literature on him, because for a long time they were attributed to the architect Francesc Berenguer i Mestres. Indeed, at first sight the building does not seem to be a typical Gaudí creation. Although the combination of undressed stone and brick passages bears some resemblance to Gaudí's buildings of the 1880s and 1890s, this stone combination was no invention of Gaudí's. He simply used it to decorate buildings, thus doubling up the pure construction material used as the ornamentation of the houses.

PAGE 207 · Archway leading to the inner courtyard. The turret is actually a chimney, the duct of which leads to a fireplace in the older part of the building.

LEFT · Described as a wine cellar, the building contained three apartments, a space for horses or motor vehicles and – right at the top – a chapel with a view out to sea. The wine cellar itself is set a little lower down, to the right of the inner courtyard, to which it is connected by small gable.

The building, known as the cellar, contained three apartments, space for horses or motor vehicles and – right at the top – a chapel with a sea view. In formal terms, this building is totally out of keeping with Gaudí's other works; even the very imaginative buildings of his early phase, inspired by Moorish architecture, bear no resemblance to it. And yet there are Gaudían structures everywhere: for example, the frequent use of parabolic arches – in the form of highly modern window arches, the entrance gate and a bridge that leads up to a mediaeval tower.

The roof also bears Gaudí's trademark – again not in terms of outward appearance, but in its very structure. "Sunshade and hat in one" is what Gaudí said he wanted his roofs to be, a principle put into perfect practice in the Casa Batlló. In the bodegas he went one step further. He planned the whole building with the arch-like shape of the roof as his starting point. On one side it almost reaches the ground. The building is thus given the character of a tent, and has been compared with Far Eastern pagodas.

The interior space is particularly ingenious. Moving upwards through the building, the floorplan becomes ever smaller and a certain degree of subterfuge was required to use the available space. Normally, the spaces on the upper floor would have served as passageways because the structure was too narrow to accommodate a hallway running along the side. Gaudí built an exterior balcony leading out from the house and along the wall before re-entering the building. And because it was only lit by small slits in the wall it looked like a fortified tower set inside the building, and the view from the outside gave no indication of what was happening within. The chapel right on the top floor, with an impressive view out to the sea, is reached by an outside flight of steps

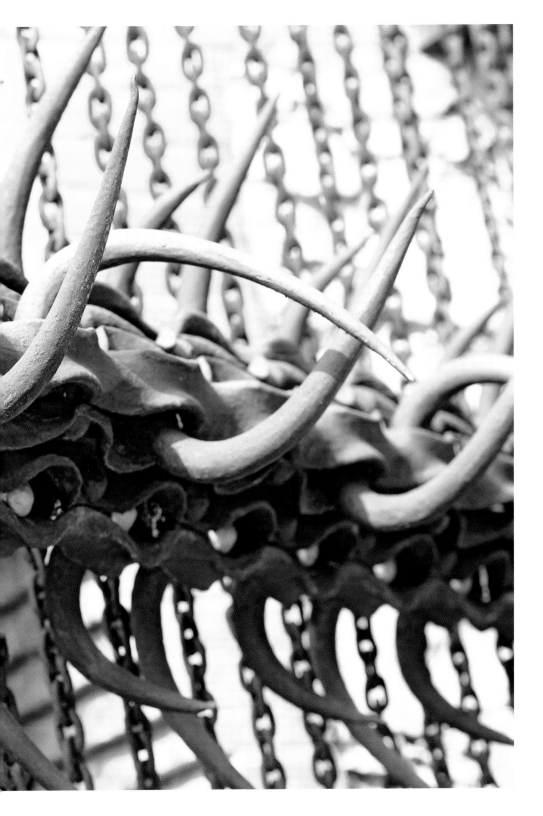

RIGHT · The entrance is not entirely the product of Gaudí's hand. The brick building was added later by Francesc Berenguer, who worked with and for Gaudí.

BELOW · Floor plan of the upper storey.

leading from the terrace to the first-floor apartment which faces the sea. A walk from the courtyard up to the top of the building takes the visitor on a rich and varied architectural tour, but still does not shed much light on the many different styles adopted. When Le Corbusier visited the property in 1928, it is hardly surprising that he saw it as a particularly illuminating example of "the learned game ... of forms assembled in the light" that characterises true architecture.

The porter's lodge contains a further characteristic feature of Gaudí's work. The archway over the entrance is closed by a gate of iron chains, which, although not as large as the Dragon Gate of the Güell estate, is nevertheless of considerable size. Just like the Dragon Gate, it is only hinged on one side, which makes it higher than the other. The basic shape of the gate is also the same as its dragon-like counterpart.

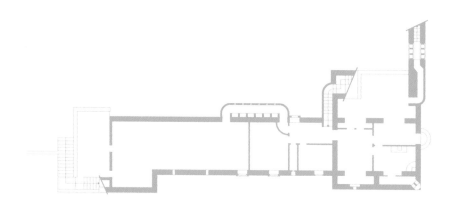

LEFT · The bell on the roof was named after Eusebi Güell's wife, Isabel

ABOVE · View of the sea from the chapel anteroom. The arched ceiling supports have been rotated by 45 degrees, creating a precisely calculated feeling of lightness.

ABOVE · The altar in the attic chapel.

RIGHT · In this historical photo, the room leading to the chapel on the top floor shows columns entwined with leaves. However,

these must surely have been decorations added for the occasion rather than plants growing on the balcony. The chapel could only be reached by the flight of steps outside, or from the balcony visible on the left.

FOLLOWING SPREAD · View from the road which now reaches right up to the building.

CASA CALVET

Calle de Caspe, Barcelona

Gaudí indeed made a name for himself as a master of magnificent, lavish works; yet most of his architectural creations were surprisingly small and often served quite trivial purposes. The Casa Calvet was to serve as both commercial premises and a residence. Perhaps this is why Gaudí displayed such reserve in designing it – the Casa Calvet (in the Calle de Caspe in Barcelona) is his most conventional work. And it was precisely for this building that he received a prize from the city; it was the only official recognition he ever received. Perhaps the building authorities were relieved that, in designing this house situated in the middle of Barcelona's elegant residential district, Gaudí had refrained from the architectural extravagances that characterised his previous works. Nevertheless, a bit of eccentricity found its way into this work: the heads of three saints on the upper floor look defiantly down – they are richly decorated hoists – and the height of the house exceeded the officially prescribed limit.

Gaudí began work in 1898 on the structure at 52, Calle de Caspe (today, the house number is 48), a residence of considerable dimensions. It was not his first attempt at this genre. In the early 1890s he had constructed a large combined commercial and private villa for Don Mariano Andrés González Luna and Simón Fernández in León which, in terms of its purpose, was quite similar to the new project in Barcelona: commercial premises in the lower part, with apartments from the first floor upwards. The house in León contained two larger and four smaller flats. The building is imposing in size and looks impressive, not really like a private home, but rather more like a palace. The neighbourhood had something to do with this: immediately adjacent to it – the Casa Botines – was the palace of the Guzmanes. Gaudí took this into consideration somewhat by adding to the sides of the building rounded oriels which rise upward like towers and, owing to the tapered, round roofs, add an intriguing touch to the otherwise more matter-of-fact overall roof design. In León, moreover, Gaudí had the option of constructing a house that stood on its own – something which could not be taken for granted in the city – and bordered the Plaza de San Marcelo on two sides.

In the Calle de Caspe in Barcelona the conditions were much less favourable than in León. Gaudí had to fit the building into a row of existing structures without leaving any gaps. This was a new experience for him, as even on the Casa Vicens project, a building closed in on all sides, he had been able to create a significant amount of room space by a shrewd division of the area he had to work with. This made the house look larger and more spacious than it actually is. By comparison, the Casa Calvet (named after the patrons, the heirs of Pere Màrtir Calvet) is almost delicate in appearance. It is squeezed in tightly between the houses on either side. And,

ABOVE · The sculpture on the edge of the roof is St Genesius of Rome.

RIGHT · With the false double gable, the building exceeded the permitted height. This meant Gaudí risked being obliged to win over the building authority, although this was one of the most conventional features of the entire building.

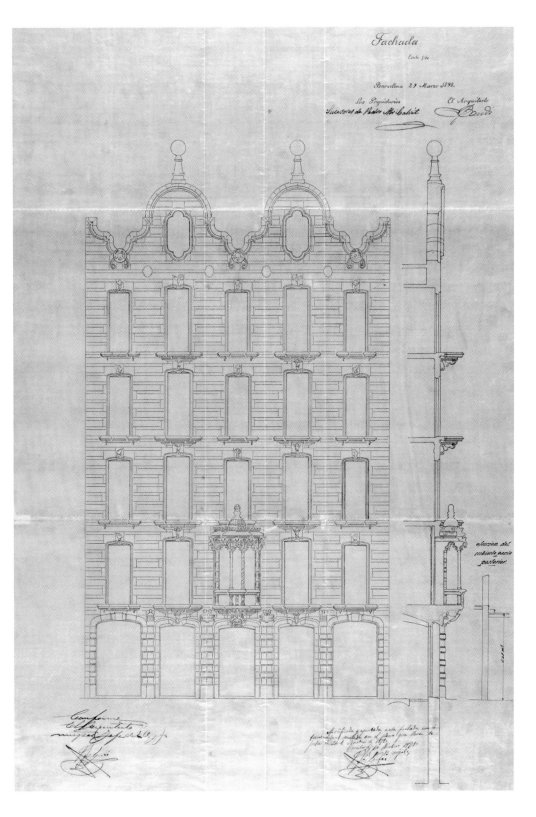

Fachada

Barcelona 29 Marzo 1898.

Los Propietarios
Sucesores de Pedro M. Cabrit

El Arquitecto

owing to the conditions of the site, Gaudí in fact immediately ran into difficulties with the neighbours. The nuns living in the convent close by had a provisional court injunction put on the building work, whereupon Gaudí put up a "screen" in the inner courtyard shielding the work from vision, thus again showing how practically minded he was. The "screen" blocks almost everything from view and yet allows an amazing amount of light to come in through numerous, carefully designed holes: the holes are shaped at the top like flattened arches, creating the effect of shutters.

Despite the relatively limited amount of space available, the house was meant to accommodate many different purposes. The cellar and ground floor were to serve, much the same as in León, as storage space and business premises. The upper floors were to contain eight apartments. Accordingly, Gaudí built – unlike in León – more upwards than outwards. Four floors rise above the ground floor. In order to find room for all the designated purposes, Gaudí designed what by his standards was a very simple building, with a nearly symmetrical floorplan. Two, almost square, equally large inner courtyards meet at the stairwell; two further oblong courtyards are situated on the sides. Their function is above all to provide light for the flats.

The Casa Calvet is certainly the most conventional of all Gaudí's works and, in terms of its overall structure, almost boring. The fact that he came into conflict with the municipal building authorities because of it is something of a tragic irony. The top of the building has two elegantly crafted gable tops which, however, overshot the maximum height for which permission had been granted. Even in the case of this relatively austere building, this feature was surely an expression of Gaudí's perpetual strokes of wit, or of perpetual obstinacy, for he could have easily dispensed with the gables; they are ornamental additions like the little towers on the Casa Vicens or the superfluous arabesque tower of El Capricho. Gaudí was also obstinate in his manner of dealing with this conflict. Whereas he had found an expedient means of dealing with the protests of the neighbouring nuns, he would not budge an inch for the authorities. He threatened to simply cut off the façade exactly at the legally prescribed height; any modification of the design was out of the question. He got his way in the end, and in fact even "topped" it all off with two crosses, lending the otherwise plain rectangular building a certain lightness, an upward thrust. In fact, he applied all of his creative energy to the design of these upper sections. The heads of three martyrs gaze down from the gables onto the street. He also used the gables to attach an extremely useful hoist which can be employed to lift furniture.

It was in keeping with Gaudí's obstinate manner that he situated all of these elements so high up the building that they are hardly visible from the street. When the Güells stopped by one day to look at the building during the construction work, Güell's wife asked unabashedly what the peculiar "snarls" up on the roof were supposed to be; Gaudí answered in his usual brooding manner that those were crosses, indeed "snarls and, for many people, a source of irritation".

Less conspicuous, but no less impressive in effect is the overall design of the façades. The Casa Calvet looks much larger than the austere, straight buildings surrounding it – not only because of the two gables on top. This may have something to do with the many balconies and their rounded, barrelling ironwork, which make it seem as if the whole façade of the house were bulging forth. Gaudí must have deliberately set out to achieve this effect, for although the Casa Calvet as a whole is almost

ABOVE · It is interesting to note the doorknocker is shaped like a louse, a symbol of everything evil. The message is that each guest is symbolically a fellow campaigner who seeks for what is good in the world.

RIGHT · Two adjacent light wells ensure that the staircase is sufficiently well lit without additional artificial lighting.

CASA CALVET

symmetrical, the balconies are of various designs. Those along the sides are smaller and also not as bulging as those in the middle. Moreover, he placed a huge oriel above the main entrance in the middle of the building that was almost baroque in design. This is the most manifest example of his predisposition to symbolic allusion, which was to take its clearest form in the Sagrada Familia. The family coat of arms adorns the entrance, as does a cypress tree, the symbol of hospitality.

But the house also derives volume from the use of a material – large blocks of undressed stone – which Gaudí had previously employed only in combination with other materials. The irregular surface of the large stone blocks prevents the façade from appearing flat, an impression which, because of the plain design, could have arisen quite easily. Here, too, much can be gleaned from drawing a comparison: in this building, with its pronounced symmetrical structure, it would not have been un-usual for the design of the rear façade to match that of the front. And in principle, this is also the case. However, instead of the roundish, bar-relling balconies, there are two rows of galleries enclosed in glass (with double-paned shuttered windows to shut out the light all the way round). This gives the façade a flat appearance, particularly as the wall sections are not made of the rough undressed stone, but are covered with smooth stone. These little deviations from the overall style are proof of the mas-ter of detail, who also took the preferences of the respective sponsor into consideration. The martyr figures below the gables are a case in point: the owner's patron saint, St Pere Màrtir, as well as the patron of Calvet's birthplace (albeit not visible from below) are both situated next to St Peter. Gaudí's love of meaningful and symbolic detail is also evident from the relatively reserved use of decoration on the front façade. On the

ABOVE · Item of oak furniture.

RIGHT · Wall mirror in the hallway.

CASA CALVET

BELOW · Desk from the chief executive's office.

RIGHT · Oak desk chair from the chief executive's office.

CASA CALVET

The textile company's former
showroom with large stained-
glass windows overlooking
the rear courtyard.

first floor, which comprised the owner's apartment, there are mushroom motifs; Calvet loved to gather mushrooms and knew them well. The entrance is also symbolic in design. Next to the cypress adorning the protruding oriel over the entrance, the doorknocker takes the guest by surprise with a particularly pithy motif: the knocker beats on the back of a louse, which stands for evil. In other words, with every knock, the visitor punishes and conquers evil before setting foot in the house.

The design of the interior also holds surprises in store, but these are less conspicuous. The spiralled pillars in front of the staircase look extravagant, but are relatively thin and reserved; they are not made of real granite – even if they look as if they are. On the other hand, the tiled wall of the stairwell is indeed remarkable and contrasts with the pillars. Its bright blue, swirling adornment reminds one of illustrations by William Blake, who as a forerunner of art nouveau, had influenced the ornamentational devices which the latter was to employ. It is not so much the overall architectural design that is impressive about this house, even though the two smaller inner courtyards were innovative at the time: Gaudí incorporated them as additional rooms into the house's design by having both lead out directly onto the stairwell. What makes the house intriguing is its "furnishings" in the broad sense of the word. These would include the impressively designed doors, whose large dark brown surfaces provide a restful atmosphere. It would also include small details such as the metal peep-holes, which Gaudí himself designed – he bored his finger into soft plaster and gave the mould to smiths to use as a pattern.

The building stands out from Gaudí's previous works for yet another reason: as in the Güell Palace, he himself designed the furniture for the patron's main living area. Fortunately, the current owner is taking care

BELOW · Ground plan of the third floor. The stairs in the centre encircle the elevator.

RIGHT · The balcony balustrades on the austere and functional rear façade look almost anachronistic.

to preserve not only the house in its original state, but in particular the furnishings. Art nouveau was the primary influence on Gaudí's furniture designs. At the same time, Gaudí also designed the chairs and seating to fit the general character of the house – plain overall, but imaginative and functional in detail. Compared with the lavishly decorated and overly elaborate furniture of the Güell Palace, these chairs and chairbacks look understated. Occasionally the lines of the backs are interrupted, and the legs are given an elegant sweep downwards. Frequently, large, almost unembellished surfaces create a surprising effect, but look pleasantly flowing and organic, while lacking in even the faintest resemblance to the surface texture of animals or plants.

In this way, the furniture repeats the fundamental characteristic of the house: the interplay of sobriety and a baroque fullness of form, whereby neither of the two ever gains the upper hand.

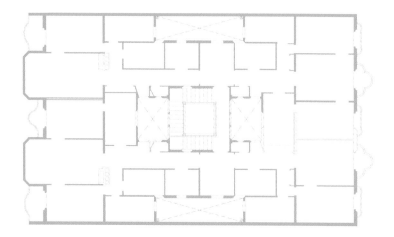

CASA CALVET

GÜELL COLONY CRYPT

Calle de Claudi Güell, Santa Coloma de Cervelló

It was originally intended to be a church. There exist two drawings in Gaudí's hand but they show practically no details. Gaudí relied on his own inspiration in the course of its construction. He was full of such ideas – a reason why he did not manage to complete most of his buildings himself. The crypt however, was left so far from completion that it is necessary to consult his drawings in order to gain even a vague idea of how Gaudí conceived this magnificent work. There are unmistakable similarities with his *magnum opus*, the Sagrada Familia. However, all that one can see at the site today – situated in the middle of the workers' settlement Santa Coloma de Cervelló – is the part, which, in the case of most churches, is usually hidden from view: the crypt. Yet even this fragment is itself so ingenious that it ranks among Gaudí's masterpieces.

GÜELL COLONY CRYPT

PAGE 245 · The fragment of the
tower makes it obvious that
the viewer is standing in front
of an unfinished torso.

LEFT · Gaudí based his sketches
on photos of hanging models of
the church.

It took Gaudí longer and longer to design and carry out his architectural projects, and he gradually deviated from the common practices of an architect – and not only in terms of style. His works since the turn of the century seem to be stations in a continuous process of reflection. The crypt marks the beginning of this development and it was the only section of what had been planned as a large church to be built. If only for this reason alone, it must be seen in relation to the large-scale project which occupied an increasing amount of Gaudí's time and energy – his work on the Sagrada Familia, where work was then progressing quite swiftly.

Gaudí's friend Güell had set up a textile factory in 1898 and opened a workers' settlement directly adjoining it. It was located south of Barcelona in Santa Coloma de Cervelló. This is why Gaudí's contribution to the settlement has been classified under a variety of names in the relevant literature: as the crypt of the Güell Colony, as the church in Santa Coloma – a somewhat euphoric and all too optimistic characterisation, for all that exists of this "church" is the lowermost part, the base of no more than a fragment of the whole building; it is also referred to as the Güell chapel, as the Güell church, or simply Santa Coloma. The multitude of different names is at times a source of confusion.

The original plan did, in fact, call for a church; Gaudí's sketches give a rough idea of how this might look, but nothing more than that. Rather, Gaudí's drafts for this building, like those of the Sagrada Familia, create more of an overall impression, conveying the desired atmosphere. And indeed they are not completely without interest, not so much with regard to the church which was planned for the colony, but rather because its style anticipates that of the Sagrada Familia. For example, the church in the drawings is topped by a whole series of towers, such as the admittedly

more slender and sharper ones that were later to become part of the Sagrada Familia. It also contains the parabolic arch design, which appeared for the first time in the lobby of the Güell Palace. The lower part of the church follows a horizontal, broadly sweeping, wavy line of the same type that recurs in the roof of the Sagrada Familia parish school. It also bears similarities, incidentally, to the winding bench in Güell Park. The third basic design component anticipated in the church is a series of slanting pillars used as a foundation; they too recur in Güell Park, which was made at about the same time as the crypt. Both architectural creations belong to one and the same stage of development in Gaudí's design.

It is almost impossible, however, to imagine today how the church was ever to rise up above the crypt. The crypt hugs the upper part of a small hill covered with pine trees, making it inaccessible from behind. In front of the crypt there is a large vestibule supported by pillars. It is difficult to see how these two elements together could serve as the foundation of a large church building. However, Gaudí was always full of surprises, which usually came to light after the fact; it was not until the building was completed that one could see how the individual parts fit together to make a coherent whole, both stylistically and in terms of engineering. In that sense, it is most regrettable that work on the church never got any further, and also that no plaster model was ever made of it;

GÜELL COLONY CRYPT

the model made for the Sagrada Familia provided enough information to enable work on the church to proceed, even decades after Gaudí's death.

Be that as it may, Gaudí's work on the crypt of the church could not have proceeded without a model, which, however, was not a model of the finished product, but one that served as a basis for structural calculations. Gaudí worked for more than ten years on this little crypt – a long time, only warranted if one regards the design plans as a preliminary step in the large-scale Sagrada Familia project. Indeed, the crypt provided Gaudí the structural engineer with a field for experimentation, an opportunity to develop the two underlying structural components of his buildings to the full: the already familiar parabolic arch and the slanted pillar. Together with his assistants and colleagues, Gaudí designed a model in which he could assess the respective pressure which would have to be borne by the arches and pillars: he suspended little sacks filled with buckshot from a network of strings, and the sacks corresponded to the respective weights (at a ratio of 1:10,000) which he assumed the arches and pillars would have to support. In this way, the strings formed a structural model of the building, albeit on its head. If the photograph of the model is turned upside down, one can see the structure of the planned building. In other words, Gaudí did not draft a design on the drawing board, but studied the static forces in nature, or at least used a model which replicated the natural ratios.

There is no sign of this in the crypt, of course. Gaudí only studied a model for the project. However, the completed work quite clearly exhibits the results which were achieved by using the model. The pillars are the first thing that catches the eye. Gaudí employed his usual material – bricks, including rounded bricks to some extent, which he arranged

ABOVE · View of the entrance from the lower part of the vestibule.

LEFT · Ground plan of the pillared hall leading to the entrance of the crypt, with parts of the roof structure and supporting columns.

to have specially made. This material was complemented with basalt, large pieces of which he put together to form pillars. He then joined the roughly hewn blocks of stone at the seams with lead. When one slowly approaches the centre of the crypt, i.e. the altar, the first reaction is to duck. The pillars slant so sharply that one cannot help thinking that the structure they support will collapse at any moment. Contrary to his usual custom, Gaudí deliberately did not use brick for the central supporting pillars, but large blocks of basalt instead. Perhaps he chose this design to avoid heightening the already fragile sense conveyed by the vaulted ceiling.

However, this chancel is not really a vault. Rather, Gaudí designed the ceiling here, as he did in Bellesguard, with numerous arches masoned in bricks. This makes the room appear lighter towards the top; the ceiling does not seem to bear down so heavily on the columns. The light basalt columns and the brick columns, the bottom third of which are plastered over, enhance this impression. The overall feel is of something that looks less like the product of human hands and more like a cave into which the ceilings have merely been carved, thus making the visitor feel as if they were standing in a large vault. No two elements in the construction are identical. No one pillar is like another, just as no one tree trunk in nature is like another. As a matter of fact, the crypt and Güell Park, which dates from the same period, are the two works by Gaudí which come closest to nature, although he did not by any means attempt to imitate nature. He only incorporated elements already present in it, which of course included structural elements. The stairs leading to the crypt (and originally intended to lead to the entrance of the church per se) reveal the degree to which Gaudí was guided by nature. An age-old pine tree stands on the site of the crypt and other architects would surely have had it felled without a second thought. Gaudí, however, left it where it was and simply ran the stairs around the tree. It does not take much time to build stairs, he mused, whereas a tree needs much longer to grow. The irregular winding stairs which took shape as a result give the impression of leading around the crypt and enhance the natural aura of the building as a whole.

The chancel itself, which draws the visitor's eyes towards the sacred core (the brick arches meet like spokes in a wheel above the altar), is encircled by a U-shaped hall, which actually contradicts the nature of the crypt. At this point the visitor's gaze is held by a veritable thicket of pillars; unlike the nave of the Sagrada Familia, the pillar design of which resembles a forest, the Güell Colony Crypt is marked by irregularity, even primitiveness. Above all, the pillars "branch out" in numerous angles at the top, creating a network of lines. This hall of pillars, which forms the forecourt to the crypt itself, appears to function as a gradual approach to the church. The pillars reflect the structure of a pine forest, a gradual transition from nature to architecture. The architectural principles of the hall of pillars are similar to those used in the crypt, but are all the more obvious to the observer here. This hall, strictly speaking, consists only of oversize (hyperbolical) parabolic arches and slanted walls and/or pillars. They are in themselves sufficient to bear the weight of the vaulted ceiling, which moreover also functions as the foundation for the stairs leading to the main church building. Here the ceiling functions as both ceiling and floor, like the ceiling of the "Greek temple" in Güell Park, which is at once roof and supporting surface for the market square constructed on top of it.

Gaudí thus created a synthesis of supports and weights, which was to attain perfection in the pillars of the Sagrada Familia.

With this crypt design, Gaudí also achieved an ideal combination of a natural-looking exterior and ornamentation – albeit reserved (and understandably so) in comparison with Güell Park. This ornamentation consisted of mosaics which had been created by his colleague Jujol, who also designed the ornaments in the park. Here the affinity with the Sagrada Familia is manifestly evident: the mosaics include two devotional references to Joseph, the patron saint of the Sagrada Familia.

The church of the Güell Colony was never completed. The crypt with the pillared forecourt is but a small torso. And yet here Gaudí created a perfect unity. The gloomy, natural-coloured building hugs the hills and thus, in a way, forms a second, artificial slope. Architecture seems to duplicate nature. This is true all the way down to the details, as in the design of the windows, for example, which are colourful in much the same way as those of Bellesguard, but no longer bear the slightest resemblance to art nouveau forms. The crypt windows take forms entirely patterned after nature: they look like coagulated drops of liquid in which the light is colourfully refracted. Even though the crypt may be the first, small part of a large church project, it is nonetheless a perfect little masterpiece of architecture.

ABOVE · Gaudí would use canvases as part of his hanging chain models, designed to calculate the building's static equilibrium. He would then take photographs from which to develop the external design.

RIGHT · View into the crypt's main space.

FOLLOWING SPREAD · Stained-glass windows of the crypt, which look like blooming flowers; they actually emanate from the four-sided cross in the centre.

ABOVE AND RIGHT · Although they serve as a rigorously functional part of the roof construction, the brick vaults had their own decorative effect.

FOLLOWING SPREAD · Gaudí designed special pews, fashioned from wood and wrought iron and produced in the Colonia Güell's own workshops. Following Gaudí's death, the altar was positioned on one side of the crypt, whereas he would have preferred to place it in the centre.

TORRE BELLESGUARD

Calle de Bellesguard, Barcelona

Gaudí was a Catalonian in every respect. Nearly all of his works contain small references to his nationalist convictions. In 1900 he began work on a structure which became a symbol of Catalonia, the dream of a great past, a past which lay in the distant Middle Ages. Gaudí built a country manor for Maria de Sagués i Molins which would have been fitting for a mediaeval prince. The majestic gate, pointed parapets, and high tower give it the appearance of a relic from ancient times. Not only is the style reminiscent of Catalonia's great era, however, but so is the ground on which the manor was built. This was once the site of a magnificent country residence – belonging to Martin of Aragon, the last King of Barcelona. Out of a sense of reverence, Gaudí left the few remains of this old aristocratic structure untouched – a memorial to the people of Catalonia.

PAGE 271 · The lady who commissioned the project wanted a regular-sized country house, while for his part Gaudí planned a fresh interpretation of the former royal castle set among the ruins remaining on the surrounding plot of land.

LEFT · The battlements and the windows of the lower attic floor combine to create their own artistic unity. To a visitor standing directly in front of the house, the battlements along the edge of the roof, together with the relatively small windows, produce – not unintentionally – the effect of a siege castle.

Gaudí's Catalonian origins and Catalonian patriotism found expression in many of his works. It was not without reason that his friend Joaquín Torres-García called him the "most Catalonian of all Catalonians". In the houses he designed (such as the Casa Calvet and the Casa Milà, for example) one repeatedly comes across the words "Fe, Pàtria, Amor", the motto of Juegos Florales, the Catalonian writers competition. The Catalonian flag with its yellow and red stripes is also a familiar feature, as is the serpent's head of the Catalonian coat of arms (in the form of a large mosaic plate, for example, at the foot of the large staircase at the entrance to Güell Park). In 1907 Gaudí proposed erecting a sun-dial as a monument commemorating the 700th birthday of King James I the Conqueror. In 1910 he also wanted to dedicate numerous large-scale projects to honour the 100th anniversary of the birth of the Catalonian philosopher Jaume Balmes i Urpià. Neither of these patriotically inspired projects was carried out, and the government could not be expected to support such a plebeian, and nationalist way of thinking. In the end, Gaudí was only permitted to design two large street lamps in honour of Balmes, and these were removed as early as 1924. After all, Gaudí never did have much luck with public institutions. He carried out his plans and dreams for the most part with the help of private contracts. The Catalonian coat of arms in Güell Park, for example, still exists today.

His most patriotic undertaking, however, was the Bellesguard house built between 1900 and 1909. It was built at a time when Gaudí had put his initial, still developmental attempts behind him and struck out on an architectural course of his own, albeit not yet as the mature, completely self-assured architect of the Güell Park.

ABOVE · The words *Ave Maria Purísima, sin pecado concebida* – in English *Hail Mary, conceived without sin* – appear on the iron grille above the entrance.

RIGHT · Because the tall staircase is situated behind the entrance façade, the windows do not match the floor elevations.

TORRE BELLESGUARD

TORRE BELLESGUARD

Viewed purely from the standpoint of architectonic structure, the house is a transitional work. It contains old Gothic elements; the floorplan is – as in the Casa Calvet – relatively simple. It holds a special position in Gaudí's work as a whole. There are none of the touches of Moorish architecture here, none of the elegant sweeps of his art nouveau adaptations, and above all, there is none of the colour which he used to such extravagant effect in Güell Park – where he was also working at the time – and would faithfully employ all the way to the spires of the Sagrada Familia. Even though Bellesguard is not uniform in style – something one never finds in Gaudí's works – it nevertheless has the appearance of a relic of former times. It stands in the landscape like a monolithic block, an impression to which the nearly square floorplan contributes in no small way.

Were it not for the transverse cross on top of the tower, which can be seen from a distance, and which became almost a trademark of Gaudí's works – one might think one is viewing the remains of a mediaeval structure. This was not so very far removed from Gaudí's intentions.

He deliberately alluded to the Middle Ages in designing the building. The house cannot be considered a prime example of Gaudí's new, avant-garde style of architecture; rather, it is a kind of monument to the great Catalonian past. In designing the house, Gaudí drew a great deal of inspiration and guidance from the site on which it was to be built. This was entirely in keeping with the tendencies that he pursued in all his other works during this year. He arranged the overall plan of Güell Park, for example, in line with the natural conditions of the site. In the case of Bellesguard, the building arises out of the historical past of the site. Maria de Sagués i Molins, the widow of Figueras, had admired the architect for a long time and in 1900 commissioned him to design a building that would revive the historical meaning of the site on which it was to stand: it was here that in 1408 Martin of Aragon, the last King of the House of Barcelona, who was known as "the humane one", had had a country residence built. It was he who had coined the name "Bell Esguard" ("beautiful view"), a name of which the house is, incidentally, truly deserving: it is situated halfway up the hills that overlook Barcelona and provides a splendid view of the city. Ever since the reign of Martin of Aragon, Castile had taken hold of Spain's fate; the golden age of Catalonia had passed.

The manor house clearly makes use of mediaeval elements. Here one again encounters the pointed Gothic arches which he had actually already given up using. On one corner, a pointed tower, completely in the style of mediaeval (if not Gothic) palace architecture, soars above the body of this impressive building. However, these are not direct "quotations" but at most vaguely imitated elements. In this way, attention is diverted from the pseudo-Gothic windows to the large cross patterns Gaudí had put below the sills and which repeat the cross that crowns the tower.

The strict design of the façade, which reveals elements of mediaeval castle crenellations, is also reminiscent of the Middle Ages: a sharply cut parapet encircles the roof like a rampart. The building can be seen as a monument commemorating Catalonia's age of glory – something which Gaudí was not able to get away with in the public spaces of Barcelona. The small mosaics to the right and left of the main entrance can also be interpreted as a symbolic reference to history – two fish in bright blue, and above each of them, a crown – an allusion to Barcelona in former times when it had been the great maritime power (the "Council of the One Hundred", convened by King James I the Conqueror as early as 1259, decreed the "Consolat de Mar", the first maritime law of modern times, which

The three-dimensional,
four-armed cross at the top of the
tower quickly became one of
the indispensable characteristics
of Gaudí's architecture.

later probably served as a model for similar constitutions in several Med-iterranean states). The iron entrance gate – as it stands today – does not, however, correspond to Gaudí's intentions. He had designed a wooden gate that would fit in better with the austere overall castle design. On the other hand, the iron gate is in tune with the style of the manor. There is none of the elegant ornamentation that Gaudí used in other buildings. Thus, the gate's design is completely in keeping with the window-grating Gaudí created, which, owing to the rounded iron bars (as opposed to the flat iron bands usually preferred) look rigid and uninviting.

But the history of the site was also preserved outside the actual build-ing. Antoni Gaudí left the ruins of the old country manor standing, even attaching them to the newer structure by means of a garden. In order to achieve this, he altered the course of the cemetery path, which originally ran between two tower ruins. For this path he designed a colonnade of slightly slanted pillars – similar to that employed in the Güell Park.

Despite its austere, square shape, the building merges exception-ally well into the landscape. Gaudí combined his favourite material, bricks, with the slate available at the site. As a result, the building has a gloomy look about it, shot through with a fascinating mixture of col-ours ranging from shades of ochre brown to grey-black. This gloomy impression also predominates on the lower floors. Thick pillars that get wider towards the top, and which, as a result, look somewhat squat and short, support the vaulted ceiling made of brick masonry. The same feature is repeated on the first floor of the attic, but the large hall there is full of light, owing to the large windows. The mas-sive vaulted arches made of brownish, unglazed (i.e. unfired) bricks look almost ornamental, despite the unplastered stone which Antoni

BELOW · Detail of a mosaic by Domènec Sugrañes Gras, who, after Gaudí withdrew from the project, also designed the brightly-coloured mosaics for the benches on either side of the entrance.

Entrance hall and staircase
with the display of blue tiles,
later added by Sugrañes.

Gaudí preferred, true to his style of "honest" architecture that covered up as little as possible.

The upper floors of this building have an amazingly airy ambience, something one would not expect judging from the outside of the house. Gaudí achieved this not only by including a large number of windows, but also and above all by means of an element he had seldom used thus far: the white plaster finish on the walls. In this respect, Bellesguard already anticipated those future works in which light would play an increasingly important role. The plaster finish had still another function: it toned down the room's severe design, making the walls "softer" and the corners less harsh. This is the beginning of the wavy structure used in the Casa Milà. Thus, Bellesguard, which looks so straightforward at first glance, proves to be a complex of contradictions. This is also apparent if one compares the floorplan and elevation. The floorplan is almost square; only the front gate protrudes slightly; above it rises the tower (which, by the way, again alludes to the Catalonian coat of arms). The elevation is totally different. The building seems to work upwards step by step – a three-tiered ascent all the way up to the crowning pinnacle, the tower. This gives the castle a certain touch of elegance.

Apart from the basement and the large hall on the first attic floor (which looks extremely complicated, but is in fact simply based on Gaudí's principle of carrying arches), this castle-structure, which looks so heavy-set from the outside, holds all the elegance of the most beautiful art nouveau villa on the inside. The white, almost undulating plaster walls and pillars, which often branch out at odd angles, seemingly leading into other areas and floors, virtually soak up the light, intensify it, pass it on; light and shadow enter into ornamental interplay. One's view does not come to rest anywhere, is forever moved on to something else. This brings us to the question of structure. In these white-plastered upper floors, the house appears to be a single room, with numerous bulges and angles. Yet, here again, Gaudí avoids stylistic purity, even when it is a matter of his own style. He used iron bars to support thinner walls. True to his honest nature, he never covered anything up, although it would have been easy for him to do so. Thus, even these rooms, which are so harmonious, always hold surprises in store, "stones that one stumbles over", including even such charming elements as the colourful mosaic windows in which Gaudí playfully alluded to church windows. However, he divided them up into larger complexes reminiscent of art nouveau windows, thus embedding symbolic allusions in them – to Venus, the goddess of love. Gaudí combined these art nouveau windows, which seem to originate in a different world, with tiled walls in the style of the region. A surprising contrast is in store around the next corner, where the windows are austerely framed in dark wood and Gothically pointed towards the top – further evidence that Gaudí was still only playing with the historical elements of style, creating a collage of the most diverse architectural elements. However, his collage never looked like patchwork. Rather, it became a new unity – as did that of the Surrealists later – and, seen as a whole, forms the basis of a new style.

Therefore, the oddly pyramid-shaped roof is not a stylistic flaw either, despite its robust design. If one goes out onto the roof, leaving the ethereally light ambience of the attic's interior, one will see that it is really the crowning feature of the structure, even if it has a playful feel to it: a number of humorous-looking, little pointed window oriels, and especially the "mosaic" of the roof's surface, enabled Gaudí to avoid any impression of compact heaviness, which is in fact the building's basic character. The "mosaic" roof surface is

ABOVE AND RIGHT · View of the
parlour's rib-vaulted ceiling. The
style of the ribs is reminiscent of
giant water lilies as they float along.

FOLLOWING SPREAD · The lower
of the two attic rooms has a vaulted
brickwork ceiling on which rests
the room above with its stone roof.

BELOW · Ground plan of the first floor. The observation tower rises above the protruding entrance hall.

RIGHT · The roofscape is accessed via a narrow door next to the tower. It spirals around several times before reaching the top of the roof.

only made of undressed stone, but looks astonishingly full of variety and liveliness since Gaudí used the widest variety of stone. Moreover, the roof fits harmoniously into the colour of the landscape. Only the pointed tops of the gallery wall that runs round the roof return us once again to the period which Gaudí wished to invoke with his "Beautiful View" – the Middle Ages, the period in which, in the year 1409, Martin of Aragon married Margarita de Prades at Bellesguard. And it is no coincidence that Gaudí, proud Catalonian that he was, stopped working on this project exactly 500 years after that event, even though he had not completely finished it. Bellesguard is one in a long list of works which Gaudí never finished; it was not until 1917 that Domènec Sugrañes Gras completed it.

GÜELL PARK

Calle de Olot, Barcelona

Dense pine forests, magnificent avenues lined with palm trees – nowadays, the tract of land in the north-west of Barcelona is indeed what its name promises, namely a park. Where once upon a time retirees could meet for a quiet chinwag and young couples for an intimate tête-à-tête, the park is no longer open to the public unless, like thousands of tourists, they pay to get in. The brightly coloured, undulating bench, which winds its way around the park like a giant snake, is now the main attraction in what has now become a theme park. When Gaudí started work here, however, there was no trace of a park. There were no springs, the land was barren, the slopes bereft of all vegetation. It is Gaudí who must be thanked for the trees and bushes which now grow here. But a straightforward park, a recreational centre for Barcelona's inhabitants, is not what was originally planned. Eusebi Güell, Gaudí's most ardent admirer and sponsor, had intended something that went further: he had planned an exemplary suburban colony, a paradise of homes, a town of gardens. Yet a park is what emerged – to the benefit of all Barcelona.

In actual fact, the name of the monumental formation, which has taken its place in both Barcelona's landscape and Gaudí biographies – the Güell Park – is an understatement. Admittedly, the area now serves as a municipal park and was planned as such by Eusebi Güell – it was meant to become the second-largest park in the city. Güell probably had the idea while travelling abroad; above all, the English landscape gardens had appealed to him, intended as they were to counterbalance the increasing industrialisation of the cities. The example set by the more organic Romantic gardens also most assuredly played a role in the project, with their well-kept ambience that nevertheless bears the stamp of natural vegetation.

This great undertaking can be seen as an extension of the sense of social commitment that had earlier led Gaudí to collaborate on the project for a workers' settlement in Mataró. Güell devoted much of his attention to the ideas for social reform that were blossoming in the England of the day(it is clearly no coincidence that Karl Marx was compiling his theoretical works in London at the time). Güell, at any rate, certainly did not wish to have a private park, even if a perimeter wall was part of the plans from the outset. The latter was meant to give the inhabitants of the area a sense of security, for at the time when it was conceived and built, the park was some distance from the city. Today, the situation has changed. The park was not created to serve as a recreational paradise or as an excursion resort for city-dwellers, but as a suburb, admittedly for persons with somewhat higher aspirations and not exactly without means. Sixty triangular allotments were foreseen for this purpose; they were meant to be situated on an expansive, steep slope so that the buildings would not mar the view of the city. All the sites were to be in areas that caught the sun.

Photo of the Park in 1915. On the left of the picture the great hypo-style hall can be seen, as can the bench, still under construction.

The as yet young plants can hide neither Gaudí's work in progress nor the finished constructions.

Both buildings at the entrance –
in this case the porter's lodge
– had small terraces on their
upper stories.

The plan failed miserably. Only two allotments were sold and the city showed no interest in the magnificent enterprise. Gaudí himself moved into one of the two houses; not, however, because he wished to live in a stately home – in this respect he was unassuming and became ever more modest the more he immersed himself in his work. In the closing years of his life he even moved into the builders' workshop at the foot of the slowly emerging Sagrada Familia. This was an almost symbolic act, although undertaken purely for practical reasons. Yet, until then it was Güell Park that had been his home. Gaudí thus, in a way, became a neighbour of his great friend, for the old family residence of the Güells was already in the area occupied by the park – the building now houses a school. Gaudí moved into the house because his 93-year-old father, whom he looked after, was no longer able to climb stairs. The architect was already leading the life of a perennial bachelor, caring only for his father and sister's daughter, who lost her mother at an early age. The niece's father was a heavy drinker, unable to guarantee the girl a good upbringing or education. Yet, for all his generosity and good nature, Gaudí could nevertheless be quite a difficult compatriot: he did not, for example, tolerate couples courting in his park.

It is a shame that this magnificent undertaking failed, for Barcelona would have thus brought a settlement model into being that even today would still be pioneering. Gaudí succeeded in his plans in creating a perfect combination of settlement and recreational areas. He had foreseen a sort of "marketplace" at the centre of the site, as a meeting place for the inhabitants and as a venue for theatre and folklore performances.

The "social program" – mainly Güell's idea – failed, though not that part of the plan for which Gaudí was responsible. Except for two houses,

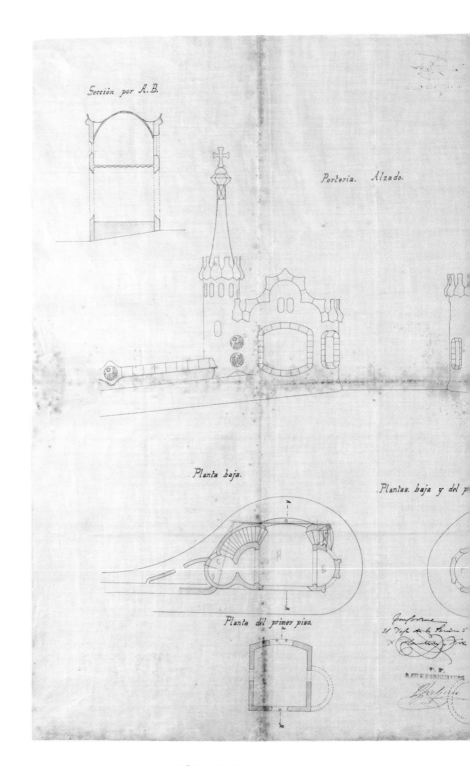

Sección por A.B.

Portería. Alzado.

Planta baja.

Plantas. baja y del p

Planta del primer piso.

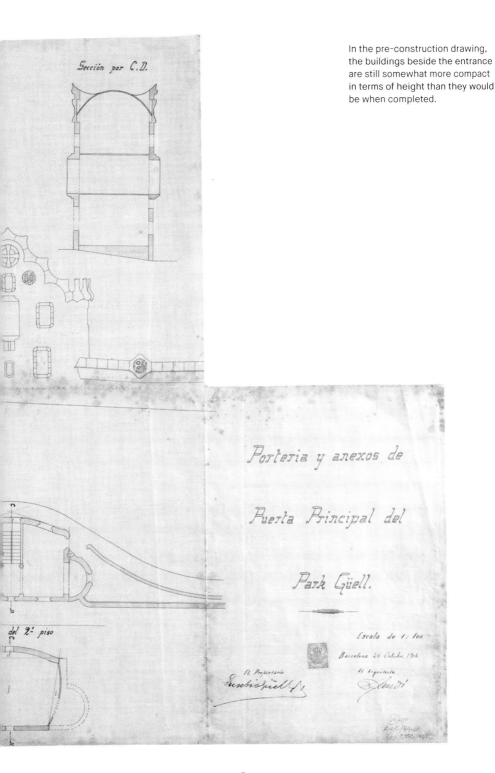

Sección por C.D.

del 2ᵈ piso

Portería y anexos de

Puerta Principal del

Park Güell.

Escala de 1: 100

Barcelona 26 Octubre 1906

El Propietario

El Arquitecto

In the pre-construction drawing, the buildings beside the entrance are still somewhat more compact in terms of height than they would be when completed.

the area originally intended as a housing estate remained free of buildings. In contrast, the recreational area has blossomed forth as a work
of art, a sort of giant three-dimensional monument, as if a sculptor had
taken a whole hill as the raw material for a figure. And what a sculptor
he was! A man with an unwavering sense of form and colour, a sculptor
who at the same time was a painter. Only in the Casa Milà did Gaudí's
ability to create sculptures of gigantic proportions take on a more incisive appearance.

As is so often the case in Gaudí's work, the park comprises highly
differing and mutually exclusive elements. Thus, the eye encounters a
wealth of bright, garish colours – which, strictly speaking, should not be
part of the overall landscape. Yet they fit into it harmoniously, enriching
it without disturbing. The same impression is left by the infinitely long
wall that surrounds the whole park, which totals some 50 acres! The wall
really is an alien body, particularly as it is partly coloured. However, it
hugs close to every twist and turn in the hilly landscape, merely repeat-
ing the contours of the earth.

Here, Gaudí adhered to the principles of English landscape garden-
ing, following the wishes of his employer, Güell, patron of the construction
work. And yet his landscape architecture is fundamentally different from
the English example on which it was modelled. As was the case with his earlier buildings – which had a sense of the Moorish about them – here Gaudí
utilises only a few of the principles culled from the model, linking them
with his own language of forms and thus creating something completely
new. The same is true of his neo-Gothic and art nouveau "borrowings".

Güell acquired the Muntanya Pelada – in the north-west of Barcelona – as the land on which to site the park. The land was almost barren

of all vegetation – and one could be led to suppose that this would actually provide perfect conditions for a new design. However, the lack of water and the stony, dry earth made the area somewhat unsuitable for a settlement – and in particular for a park with which in the first instance one associates areas of greenery. Gaudí, practically minded as ever, came up with an ingenious solution to this problem. The land in part slopes steeply, which entailed further problems for construction work. However, this hilly terrain provided the ideal conditions for a winding perimeter wall. Gaudí designed the wall to fit in with the natural environment but adorned it with strong colours, above all in those places where it would inevitably attract attention, i.e. at the seven entrance gates and especially at the main entrance. Here, in the Calle de Olot, the lower part of the wall – roughly two-thirds of it in terms of height – is built of ochreous undressed stone. Towards its crest, the wall gets thicker and is topped with a winding cover, composed of a mosaic of white and brown ceramic tiles. This has a number of advantages. Firstly, the wall covering is very decorative; in bright sunlight the wall gleams. Gaudí, however, also had some very practical intentions with this construction. What was actually inferior material would have been subject to the erosion of rain had it not been protected, but because of the "ceramic skin" the walls are waterproof. At the same time, Gaudí also strengthened the wall's function as protection against intruders from outside: the rounded-off, smooth covering offers the fingers no purchase. The wall can only be scaled with great difficulty if aids are not used. Indeed, the park as a whole is a unique synthesis of practical purposes and aesthetic effect. It demonstrates Gaudí's twofold talents perhaps even more clearly than his other works do.

LEFT · Between the two symmetrically laid-out flights of steps to the hypostyle hall, there are three fountains. The highest, with its multicoloured lizard, is the most famous of the three. Behind it rises the almost temple-like market hall, which might have served as a local amenity for the garden city that was originally planned.

ABOVE · Despite being wingless, the lizard by the fountain is often described as a dragon. Over the course of a number of repairs, it has lost some of its more ferocious look. It also acts as an overflow for the underground cistern.

86 20-feet-high columns support the roof above the market hall, which in turn props up the vast terrace. Pipes running on the inside carry rainwater collected on the terrace to the cistern.

As powerful reminders of Doric columns, these structural supports would have added a touch of class to the market activities for which the space was designed.

The main entrance was designed solely in terms of aesthetic criteria. It is flanked by two pavilions that at first sight resemble houses from some magical forest. The walls seem to be irregular and look as though they have only been fused together into a house with the greatest difficulty – and the roof undulates irregularly. And yet, as elsewhere, this lack of uniformity is misleading. Pavilions and wall do indeed form a unit. The pavilions have an oval floorplan; their walls appear to grow out of the park's wall, or put differently, the pavilions resemble "insertions" into the great perimeter wall. These small houses are, like the wall, both built of ochreous undressed stone, and rendered in a similarly colourful structure of gleaming tiles. Only the 30-foot-high turret on one of the two pavilions stands out against its background. It is without function – like the tower of El Capricho – and encased in a chequerboard-like pattern of small blue and white tiled squares. Yet again, the observer would seem to be confronted by a contradiction, a breach of the landscape's harmony, but here Gaudí incorporated the colours of the background as they must appear to the passers-by on the street: the blue of the sky and the white of clouds floating by. Just as in the wall, small medallions are embedded in the pavilions with the name of the park on them: ornamental trifles, but each with a meaningful function.

The entrance area already points to the main construction principles that the visitor will then encounter throughout the park: dumbfounding effects that attract the eye as if by magic and yet embedded in a harmony that fuses everything into one unit. The impression is of expensive, brightly gleaming materials – in what is nevertheless a construction using the cheapest of raw materials. The park was almost completely built of material that was found on the actual site, and quite a lot

GÜELL PARK

was found indeed. The terrain was too steep for roads and paths. Gaudí decided not to have parts of the hill levelled; he wanted to subject his architecture utterly to the dictates of the existing landscape. He thus designed the streets in the form of viaducts and caverned passages. In this manner he obtained stone materials, including rubble, from which he then constructed his buildings. The splendid, gleaming ceramic coverings were composed by means of a collage, the "trencadís": he procured waste, rejects, slivers and chips from good ceramic workshops, which were then pressed into the mortar while this was still soft. Thus, at the beginning of the century he had already pre-empted an art movement that was to first blossom forth in the '20s: the collage technique of the Dadaists. If it had not been for the work of his collaborator, Josep Maria Jujol i Gibert, who was a specialist in such ceramic artworks, the overall construction might have been less sumptuous and luxurious. However, such speculations are rather pointless: architecture does not occur without collaboration, and Gaudí in particular was an ardent proponent of collective projects. Work, he once said, was the fruit of cooperation, and the latter was only possible on the basis of love. By dint of his continual presence at the construction site of the Sagrada Familia he put this theory into practice.

Gaudí was never a pure theoretician. It was his conviction that the architect's task was not to invent giant projects, but rather to make these possible. Such a view clearly accords with the great 19th-century tradition of architecture. The last decades of that century saw the dissemination of a wide-ranging pragmatism, particularly in England, where the most popular manifestation was to be found in the work of William Morris. Morris thought of himself mainly as an artist, but was

Three fountains are framed by
the long staircase. The middle one
features the head of a snake and
the Catalan flag.

in fact a furniture manufacturer – inspired moreover by thoughts of social reform. As a consequence, Morris repeatedly attempted to design
pieces of furniture of an aesthetically high standard and in such a manner that the ordinary man on the street, indeed even the working-class
man, could afford them. The intention was to upgrade everyday life aesthetically. Morris would most surely have been pleased by the basic idea
underlying Güell Park. Gaudí, in other words, embarked on his career at
a time when people were bent on overcoming the division between art
and crafts, and by extension, between art and life. Güell Park is concrete
proof that this idea is not only correct, but can be put into practice. The
fact that the city was not enthusiastic about the project also shows, however, that the public was far from ready to receive such progressive ideas
(in our age of mass production, a distance is again growing between the
two areas of art and craft).

Gaudí, with his use of trivial, and indeed pathetic means to achieve
great aesthetic effects, anticipated the ideas that brought the Cubists, particularly his compatriots Picasso and Miró, worldwide success. The utilisation of materials that were of an inferior quality and thus less durable,
however, posed great constructional problems for Gaudí, so that he had to
construct his buildings as complex structures with many different layers in
order to ensure their durability. Nevertheless, from the outside they appear
to have been moulded in one piece. For example, the superstructure of turrets on the pavilion is hollow. The walls are made up of a 2,5-inch-thick inner layer of bricks and a layer of concrete, reinforced with 0,4-inch-thick
iron rods; this was the first time Gaudí had used such a material. This is
then covered by three layers of roofing tiles and finally by an external coat
of cement in which the ceramic plates are embedded, forming the mosaic.

The whole park is constructed in a similarly ingenious manner. The form of construction – invisible to the eye – first became apparent when the city of Barcelona, which has owned the park since 1922, carried out renovation work. Such work was, incidentally, not necessary until a surprisingly late date; a hallmark of Gaudí's buildings is that they are incredibly durable, even if they look as fragile as the neat small ornamental turrets on the roofs.

What is fascinating above all is the architectonic design of that part of Güell Park which was not intended as a housing area and which thus exhibits the real quality of a park as a living space. Once the visitor has gone through the entrance, flanked on either side by the two pavilions, they are faced by a monumental flight of outdoor stairs that reminds them of the great castles of yesteryear. They can go up two parallel sets of stairs – separated from one another by a large bed of organic sculptures in stone and bordered by a low stone wall – to the central sector of the park, a sector that, from the foot of the stairs, one would not even imagine existed. Before reaching this sector, the visitor's path is blocked by a monster – in a sense, the last guardian of the park: a huge dragon covered in bright "scales" of small tiles. People acquainted with Gaudí's work are already familiar with this creature. A similar animal was already to be encountered on the Güell estate, admittedly in the form of a playful, art nouveau wrought-iron gate. As is always the case in Gaudí's later work, one must suspect a deeper, usually symbolic meaning lurking behind everything that appears to be playful on the surface. The dragon represents Python, guardian of the subterranean waters, and Gaudí thus alludes darkly to what is of immense importance for the park, but which escapes the eye: behind the dragon a concealed cistern

lies, which can contain up to 2,600 gallons of water; it was conceived of as a rainwater collector. In this manner, rainwater was channelled into the collector and stored to irrigate the barren parkland, deprived as it is of any natural springs.

A few yards further on, one meets yet another reptile – a snake's head – which also serves a symbolic purpose. Gaudí alludes here to the Catalonian coat of arms: a snake's head against yellow and red lines. Practically minded as ever, Gaudí at the same time used both reptiles as overflow valves for the cistern.

The flight of stairs itself reminds the visitor of centuries past; yet, upon climbing them, the visitor will feel as though they have been transposed into an even more distant past. An ochre-coloured hall of columns rises up like a Greek temple. The columns are – with slight differences – Doric in form. Perhaps Gaudí wanted to pay homage to his financial sponsor's enthusiasm for classical antiquity. The pillars are arranged in such a manner that they appear to stand at the intersecting points of an imaginary net. Depending on where the observer stands, the columns appear to form an impenetrable forest or a structure comprising several rows, in which all the subsequent pillars disappear behind the first row. Gaudí would, however, not have remained true to himself had he not also had some fun while designing this memorial to classical Greece. The outside columns are – true to Greek custom – slightly oblique and broaden a little towards the base. However, in Gaudí's work these features are somewhat more exaggerated than in the original Doric columns. The remaining pillars in the interior of the "hall" are all of the same size. The architectonic elements of the park always have several functions. Just as the two reptiles are ornamental, symbolic allusion and overflow valves all at once, so too are the columns not just pillars supporting a roof, while the roof is not just a roof but the floor of something else. Indeed, it would seem that the function as a roof is only secondary, for the outer side of the roof serves as the square at the centre of the whole park. This space was intended as the "marketplace" for the settlement and – also following the example of antiquity – at the same time as the site for a theatre. The whole park as it was originally planned can thus be thought of as one gigantic amphitheatre. The "audience" would not have sat in rows directly surrounding the stage, however, as these "rows" are to be found on the slope opposite the square; the "seats" would have been the settlement houses themselves. What remains of this plan is the square – without the settlement. This "Greek theatre", as Gaudí was fond of calling the square, is of quite awe-inspiring proportions: 258 x 120 feet. Only approximately half of it is built on solid ground; the other half rests on the Doric columns. Thus, the Greek hall of columns is actually only the foundations of the immensely larger Greek theatre. The pillars serve in this context not just to support the roof, but at the same time as water conduits for rainwater. Such an open space collects a large quantity of water in a relatively short period of time. The columns, as compact as they may appear, are hollow; and the floor of the Greek theatre conceals a highly complex internal network. It is absolutely flat, not inclining in any direction; as a result the water does not flow in one single direction. Gaudí developed this drainage system by copying nature, something he did frequently in his mature phase. The floor of the square is not cemented; the water can thus seep into the ground, where it enters one of innumerable collecting vessels; these resemble pipes split down the middle with small openings underneath from which the water can flow into

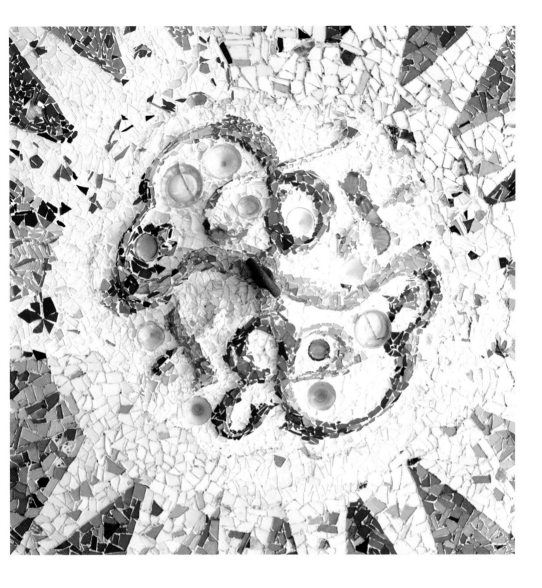

the hollow pillars. The fact that the water is also filtered during its journey into the cistern shows just how much detailed scrutiny the architect put into the design of his buildings. Small wonder that when the City of Barcelona awarded him a prize for the Casa Calvet, it was not just for the high aesthetic standard of the building, but also for his achievements in the field of ventilation and de-aeration as well as sewage removal. The symmetrical layout of the columns was, incidentally, interrupted in a few places, so that the hall did not appear over-cluttered. In the spaces

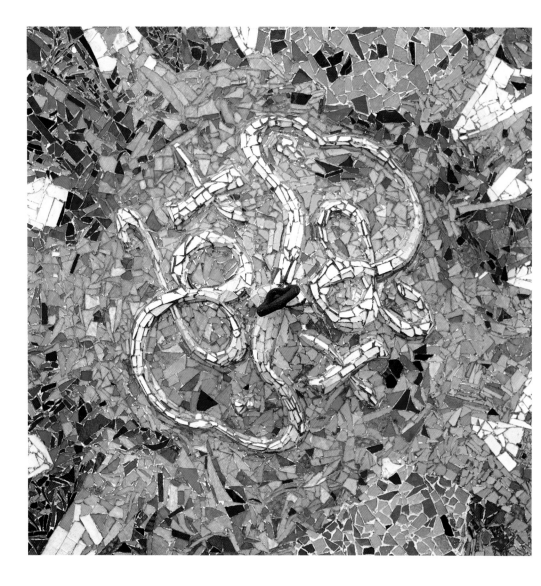

that thus remained "free" his collaborator, Jujol, installed some fascinating, large-scale medallion-like decorations.

This by no means exhausts the wealth of different functions fulfilled by this building complex. The wall surrounding the square not only serves to prevent inquisitive passers-by from falling down the steep slope, but was also designed as one long bench. The terrace thus also became a place to meet people, especially as this "endless bench" did not follow any clear, sober line. It winds its way in innumerable and highly

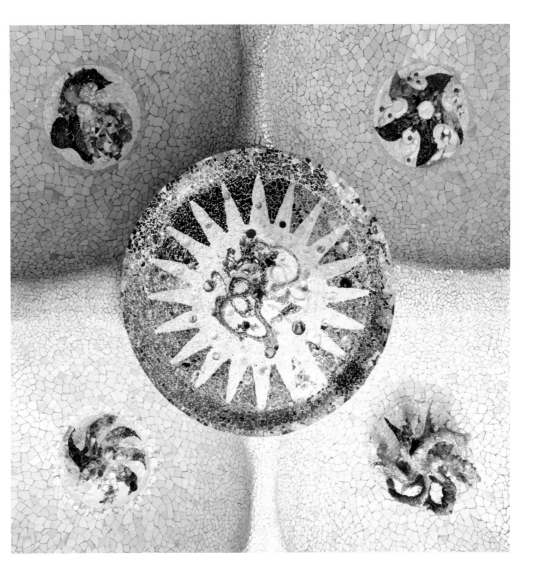

differing curves round the giant terrace. In this way it offers seating space for many people, and it is, above all, structured in such a manner that the people – although outdoors and in large number – can nevertheless form small, intimate groups in which to have a chat, as it were. It is a "chance" side effect that an organic form is thus also bestowed on the wall bench. In this phase of his work Gaudí attached greatest importance to an organic method of building. He accordingly took great pains when designing the bench to ensure that the seating and back

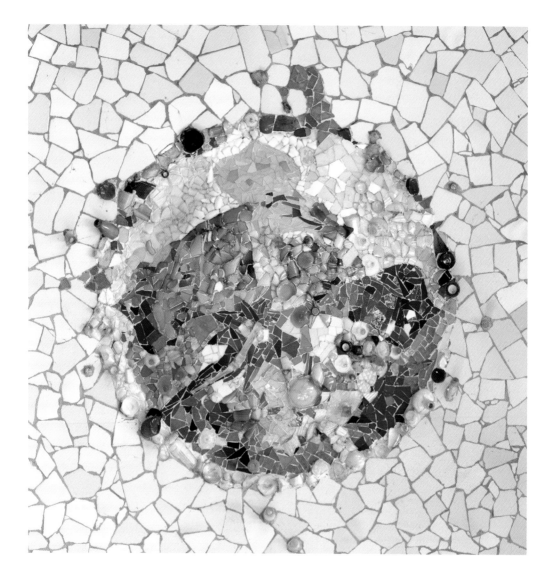

of the bench accorded with the physiology of the human body. In order
to reproduce the form of the body with the greatest precision he is said to
have sat a naked man on plaster that was still pliable, and then repro-
duced the imprint at a later stage. However abstract the ornaments on
the bench may be, they are nevertheless – as is so much of Gaudí's architecture – close to reality, "human", "natural". To ensure that one's sense
for colour did not go unheeded, he applied here what is perhaps the most
opulent and artistic utilisation of "broken ceramics". Using thousands of

broken, coloured tiles and pieces of faience, he had a mosaic created on the bench which greatly excels the decor of the roofs and walls. He relied in this context on his workers' artistic sensibilities. He could never have designed and distributed all the parts of the mosaic himself. One critic believes there is proof that the bench was decorated from right to left; if one moves in this direction, he says, one can observe an ever-increasing degree of artistic workmanship and imagination. Gaudí, as it were, created with this collective project a picture by Miró before the latter had even started painting (the work on the park lasted from 1900 to 1914; Miró was born in 1893). At the same time, the bench is both waterproof and extremely hygienic owing to the coat of mosaics.

As rich in colour as the bench is, it nevertheless does not appear out of place perhaps precisely because of its organic twists and turns which – like the park's perimeter wall – reproduce the contours of the hill. The network of roads in the park is characterised by a similar harmony with nature. If the bench is Gaudí's great accomplishment in terms of surface design, then the network of roads is his great achievement in the area of construction and structural engineering. He later based his deliberations when building the Sagrada Familia on these findings. In order to avoid any levelling of the terrain, he planned the roads in twists and turns – they run close to the edge of the incline and repeatedly pass under colonnades – as well as making use of constructions that appeared completely natural. He had the pillars made of brick as this caused only a minor optical disruption to the natural landscape. These colonnades often form caverns that seem to have evolved naturally. The slanting pillars have proved to be very sturdy, irrespective of how fragile they may appear to be. Gaudí had, after all, conducted intensive tests with models. At the

LEFT · Round, slanting pillars, following load progression along a circular route, are typical features of Gaudí's designs.

ABOVE · Strolling through the colonnades c. 1904.

same time, they provide shelter from the rain and over-bright sunlight and
are fitted out with benches that were built into the stone. Wherever possible,
if nature preordained a certain form, this was adopted in the architecture.

With Güell Park, Gaudí designed a settlement in what was until then
uninhabited terrain and at the same time paid such a great deal of attention
to preserving the natural landscape that the result could serve as a model in
our times. Indeed, in 1984 the park was placed under an international preser-
vation order by UNESCO. Architecture and nature enter a unique alliance in
the Güell Park project: the architecture not only conforms to the landscape –
it appears to have grown out of it. At first sight one frequently takes a pillar,
which culminates at the top with a flower tub, to be a palm tree (and one can
make the opposite mistake).

What distinguishes Güell Park from all Gaudí's buildings is that it exhibits the greatest proximity to nature. From this point of view, the architect
then created his later buildings: these placed a second, new nature alongside
the first nature.

CASA BATLLÓ

Paseo de Gracia, Barcelona

Mighty pillars that appear to resemble the feet of some giant elephant are the first thing to meet the eye of any passers-by from street level. The roof reminds one, however, of a completely different animal: it is bordered by a jagged line similar to the backbone of a gigantic dinosaur. A façade extends between the two, including a number of small, elegantly curved balconies that seem to stick to the front of the house like birds' nests on the face of a cliff. The façade itself glitters in numerous colours, and small round plates that look like fish scales are set into it. There are no edges or corners here; even the walls are rounded in undulations and have the feel of the smooth skin of a sea serpent about them. Salvador Dalí praised Gaudí for his *soft calf-skin doors*. In the Casa Batlló even the outer walls appear to be made of leather, soft and supple. This dream of softness and naturalness is then continued inside the building.

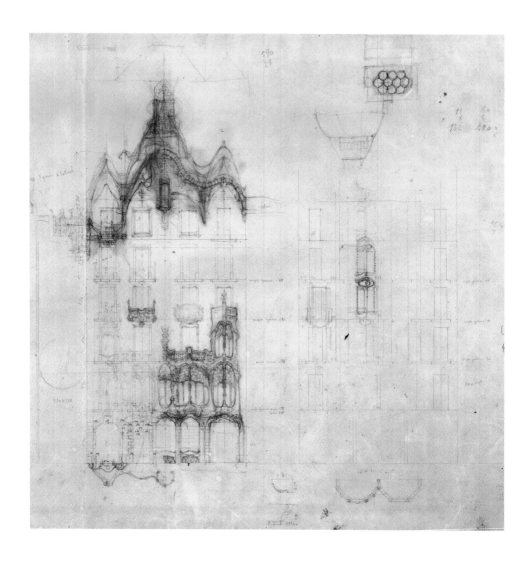

PAGE 339 · View of the top floor and the roof. The initials *JHS*, *JHP* and *M* on the turret refer to the Holy Family.

ABOVE · Because Gaudí was undertaking the reconstruction of an existing building, he sketched his design for the façade on an existing drawing.

RIGHT · Historical view from the street. To the left of Casa Batlló stands Casa Amatller. This was also a renovation of an old building, in this case the architect was Josep Puig i Cadafalch.

LEFT · The railings for the small balconies are made from a single piece of iron and immediately coated with ivory-coloured paint, so that they harmonise with the sandstone.

ABOVE · Sandstone for the details of the façade comes from a quarry on Montjuïc.

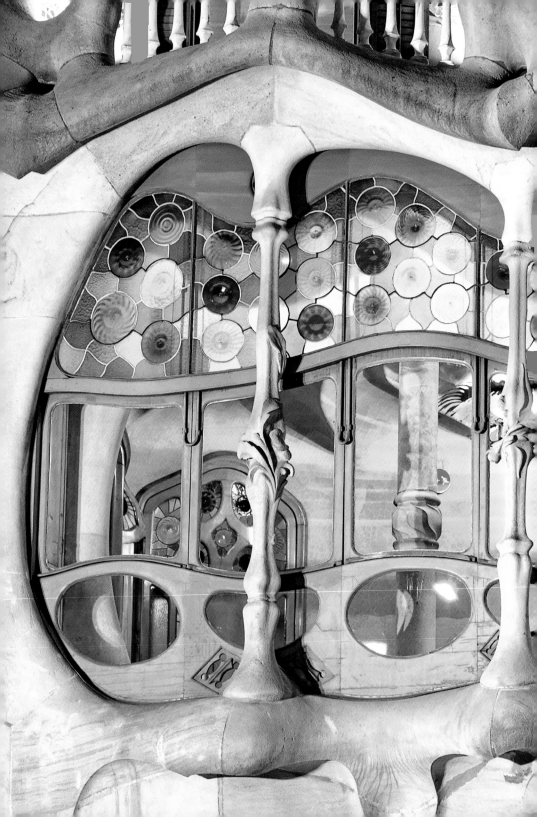

PREVIOUS SPREAD · The parlour window of the main apartment. Because the struts supporting the ceiling were set inwards from the panes of glass, a separate,

more slender, support structure was installed in front of the window to support the balconies of the floor above.

LEFT · On the street side, the animal-like hump of the soaring roof is covered with diamond-shaped, glazed brick and, on the rear side, trencadís.

There is probably no other building that better illustrates what is modern in Gaudí's work, and that does so in such a sensuous, almost symbolic manner, than this second and last of his apartment house projects. As so often, he was not able to start from scratch with the Casa Batlló but was tied to an already existing building shell. In the case of the Colegio Teresiano this had led him to introduce his conception of what the main elements of a house should be via a small number of substantial changes to the construction – impressing his mark on the house with but a few artistic tricks.

This is not the case in the narrow house in 43, Paseo de Gracia. When viewing the building today, it defies one's imagination to conceive what it once looked like. A comparison of the basic outline with the front elevation gives us an idea, however. Josep Batlló i Casanovas, a wealthy textile manufacturer, wished to completely change the appearance of his existing residence in this fashionable district of Barcelona. The apartment block had been built in 1877 and is said to have been one of the most boring and conventional houses in the district. A large number of modern buildings had arisen in the immediate vicinity. Batlló clearly wanted to outdo these buildings in terms of modernity, for Gaudí's obstinate originality in architectural design was already well known. Pere Milà, a friend of Batlló's, brought the two men into personal contact, but Gaudí is sure to have been known to the textile manufacturer. The spectacular buildings undertaken for Güell – the palace not so far away from the Paseo de Gracia, and Güell Park, which was taking shape at the time – had made Gaudí into a celebrity. And the size of the project Batlló probably had in mind can be gathered from the fact that in 1901 he applied to Barcelona's municipal authorities to have the

Four groups of chimneys – not
visible from the street – populate
the vast rooftop terrace. By far
the largest part of the roof area
remains simply as a flat roof.

old building torn down in order to erect a completely new one. However, things did not go quite that far, perhaps because Gaudí did not need such a radical break with the old. To create an utterly new building by means of but a few incisive alterations was not without its challenges. And, indeed, the building that emerged was completely new, even in terms of Gaudí's own work.

This feeling can be sensed even at the bottom of the building, which was originally very narrow at the base, but was made to seem of enormous dimensions. Gaudí's work was forever affected by the limited space of construction sites: although his buildings all appear magnificent, they are nevertheless anything but large. With a few artistic tricks Gaudí always created an illusion of magnitude. The giant iron gates achieve this for the Güell Palace. In the rebuilding of the Batlló house it was the thick pillars that he used to this end; they form an arcade around the entrance and their thickness gives the impression that the house must be of truly gigantic proportions. These pillars immediately sparked off a conflict between Gaudí and the municipal authorities. There had been objections raised by the authorities with respect to the Casa Calvet. Whereas in the latter case the bone of contention had been the height, which exceeded the permitted limits, here it was the width. The pillars jutted out a full two feet over the pavement. The pedestrians quite literally stumbled over the house – in a metaphorical sense as well. Seldom did Gaudí cause such a stir with a building as in the case of the avant-garde architecture used here. But, as with the Casa Calvet, Gaudí obviously ignored the objections raised by the authorities. The pillars, after all, are still standing. And the second attack by the civil servants also went unheeded. Inside the

LEFT AND ABOVE · The panes of glass in the inner patio become larger the further down they go, whereas the wall tiles become lighter, so as to compensate for the increasing lack of natural light. A glass roof keeps the rain out.

ABOVE · Detail of the bannister rails on the main staircase leading to the rented apartments.

RIGHT · Señor Batlló's inward-facing study, with a single window overlooking the patio.

building he had installed a mezzanine floor, and in the attic two rooms had been constructed that had not been entered on the original application for building permission. What at first sight would seem to be some formalistic argument between architect and authorities does, however, go to the very heart of Gaudí's approach. His buildings emerged in the course of construction work. This procedure assumed gigantic proportions, after all, in the case of the Sagrada Familia, yet as early as the Güell Colony Crypt unusual dimensions had arisen. Perhaps Gaudí had envisaged problems with the authorities and had thus submitted a sketch that was rich in atmosphere but said nothing about the construction at hand. But meanwhile this had become his planning method. Freehand drawings were also all the plans that were used for the crypt and the Sagrada Familia; all three are in fact quite similar.

And yet at the beginning of the construction work Gaudí had nothing to hide. The full extent of his version of the avant-garde did not reveal itself until the final stages. If one compares the building plans for the old house and the end product, then it soon becomes obvious that Gaudí actually abided quite strictly by the plan. The old house consisted, on the whole, of right-angled structures: the floorplan is repeated on each storey and the façade is dominated by four long, right-angled windows per floor. Gaudí took up this distribution of the windows, simply redesigned the forms and covered panels of the windows from scratch and supplemented these with bizarre-shaped little balconies which seem to stick to the window sills like little drops of hardened honey – and with that, a completely new type of house had come into being.

The cast-iron railings – that had themselves served as the complete balcony in earlier buildings – are supplemented, engulfed and flattered

The Batlló's private entrance to
the main floor. The skylights lead
to a small roof terrace set to one
side and shared with Casa Amatller.

by softly undulating elements of walling and plaster. There are no corners or straight lines whatsoever, as if everything were in fluid motion. And it is above all the façade as a whole that has such an effect, as if Gaudí had completely renounced the use of traditional building materials. Bricks, the material for which he had until then shown a preference, are not even used as ornaments in Casa Batlló, although this was a technique Gaudí commanded perfectly. The façade is coated in flat Montjuïc stone with the sandstone colours that have a feel of modelled clay about them – a feature emphasised by the manner in which the surface has been worked. Gaudí gave everything a wavy, undulating shape. The house has more the appearance of a gingerbread house than one made of stone. The mosaics in the façade complete this sense of standing before a magician's home. The number of ceramic components used increases towards the roof. The roof itself is covered in bluish-pink tiles on the side facing the street. The crest of the roof runs in an undulating line that traces a slight zig-zag on account of the round tiles used.

The entire house seems to be the brainchild of someone whose mind has detached itself from everything that hitherto existed and who follows only its own dreams and visions. And yet Gaudí, as was the case with many of his previous buildings, paid great attention to the surroundings of the house. The zig-zag of the roof, for example, corresponds with the strict, stepped gable of the house to the left. Gaudí also took the neighbourhood into account when deciding on the Casa Batlló's height, foregoing a fully fledged attic. In this manner the house gradually tapers towards the roof, which thus becomes a hat or a hood with a delightful little ornamental turret on one side – like a feather in a cap. This small turret is crowned by what had become Gaudí's trademark, namely the horizontal cross.

The playful impression is continued in the house's interior. Gaudí concentrated on the rooms that were going to be occupied by the owner of the building. These could not be more remote from conventional rooms. Gaudí merged everything with everything else. He had tried to do this in places in the Güell Palace, but it was not until the Casa Batlló that he succeeded in completely overcoming the usual division between rooms.

Although Gaudí followed a path of his own, it has been suggested that there are links here to art nouveau. But irrespective of the imaginative design of these rooms, they are based on a surprisingly sober structural principle. The floorplan and façade of the old house were based on a rectangular structure. In Gaudí's building these also accord with one another, the sole difference being that the underlying forms are completely new. Just as the windows look like outgrowths of plants, not one of them identical with another, so too the floorplan is determined by irregular forms. It resembles above all the "construction plan" of organic cells.

ABOVE · Vestibule of the
Batlló family's main residence.
An elliptical mirror creates
a cut-off point, making it clear
that this is a private space.

BELOW · The dining room in the Batlló's second-floor apartment whose features and furniture no longer exist. The glazed door in the centre leads to the outdoor terrace at the rear of the building.

FOLLOWING SPREAD · The parlour as it was in 1927. The cumbersome furniture of the period and the curtains that darken the room make it seem much narrower.

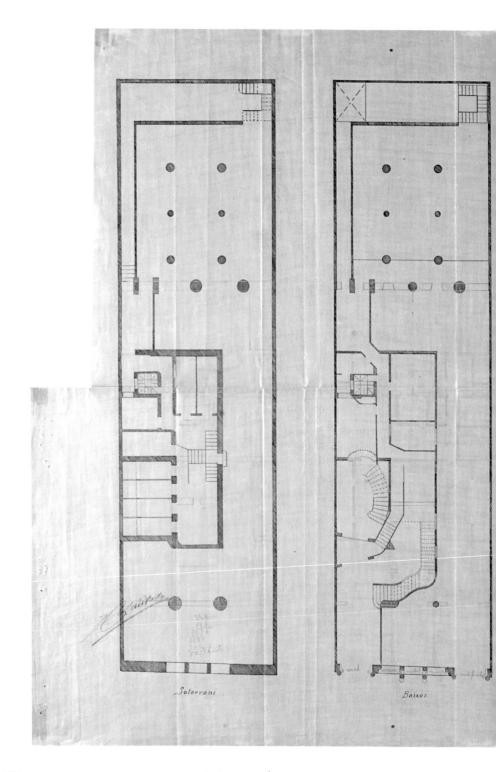

Soterrani

Baixos.

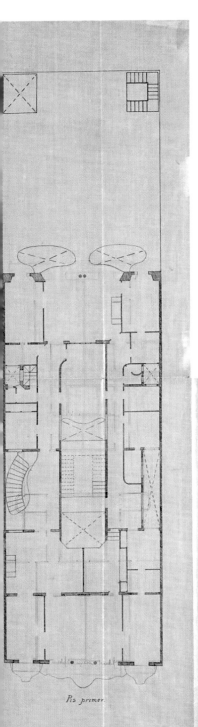

Floor plans of the cellar and the first and second floors. Gaudí's reconstruction work and additions are indicated in red.

Construcció de soterrani, pis 5.^{nt} i abitacions de servei del terrat, i reforma de la fatxada, baixos i pisos 1.er, 2.^{on}, 3.er i 4.^t de la casa n.° 43 del Passetj de Gracia, propietat de D. Josep Batlló.

Plantes del soterrani, baixos i pis primer.

Escala de 1 x 100

Barcelona 26 d'Octubre de 1904

El Propietari.   L'Arquitecte.

Pis primer.

ABOVE · Bench seats are built into the recess on either side of the open fireplace.

RIGHT · The parlour as it is today. The whirlpool effect of the ceiling conjures up thoughts of the sea.

FOLLOWING SPREAD · Pendant lights in the study. The two doors lead into the large and small parlour respectively.

LA PEDRERA

Casa Milà, Calle de Provenza, Barcelona

La Pedrera – the quarry – was the name an astounded population gave to this completely unique building. It could be compared with the steep cliff walls in which African tribes build their cave-like dwellings. The wavy façade, with its large pores, reminds one also of an undulating beach of fine sand, formed, for example, by a receding dune. The honeycombs made by industrious bees might also spring to the mind of the observer viewing the snake-like ups-and-downs that run through the whole building. In this last secular building that he constructed before devoting all his energies to the Sagrada Familia, Gaudí created a paradox: an artificial but natural building which was simultaneously a summary of all the forms that he has since become famous for. The roof sports an imitation of the bench from Güell Park as well as an ever more impressive series of bizarre chimney stacks.

PAGE 373 · View of the side entrance in the Calle de Provenza,
part of a structure that is not quite
symmetrical. All the cut stone to
be used for the façade had to be
carefully customised on site.

RIGHT · Once again, Josep Maria
Jujol was responsible for the extraordinary wrought-iron balcony
rails, each of which was different
from all the rest.

With the Casa Batlló, Gaudí had actually reached the zenith of his design of secular buildings. One can hardly conceive of a greater freedom,
a more magnificent and anarchic development of imaginative forms that
nevertheless relies on traditional house forms. What is more, in the Casa
Batlló Gaudí had perfected this new stylistic phase. In Güell Park and the
Güell Colony Crypt he had approximated nature to such an extent that
the buildings seemed to resemble a second nature, an artistic redesigning of nature's forms and construction principles. And he sublimated
this approach in the Casa Batlló. Pure art forms reminiscent of nothing but nature evolved from these near-natural forms. There is a great
deal of truth in it when the façade is compared with the surface of a
sea whipped up by a storm. The small splinters of mosaic in the façade
remind one of the foaming crests of the waves; yet, under Gaudí's hand
these become purely ornamental elements. Gaudí did not make forms
in order to copy nature. Even the furniture that he created for the house
owner was unmistakably fashioned after the human body – but Gaudí
did not use any anatomical forms. The days were over when he would
shape door-handles in such a way that they could be taken for bones. His
intensive preoccupation with nature had allowed him to assimilate its
essential underlying structures: he could now play with them at will, as
he did with the existing architectural styles when he first started design
work. He also played with elements of his own style, which became ever
clearer in this, the mature phase of his art.

With regard to the wealth of imaginative ideas, the Casa Batlló is
certainly not outclassed by the Casa Milà. The fascinating use of colour
is missing, as is the sumptuous use of different ceramic materials and
forms. And one could search in vain in the interior of this last house

LA PEDRERA

PREVIOUS SPREAD · Stone for the façade originated from different quarries. For the lower floors it came from Garraf, for the top floors it was shipped from Vilafranca. In the eaves there is a rosebud, crowned by the letter *M*. Originally, a group of figures some 13 feet tall, including the Virgin and Child and two archangels, was to have been placed there.

LEFT · Unlike those at the Casa Batlló, the superstructures on the roof of Casa Milà are easily seen from the street. They play an important role in the overall composition.

PAGE 379 · There are three
different types of superstructure –
entrances to staircases leading
from the roof, chimneys and
ventilation shafts.

RIGHT · View of the roofscape
with chimneys and, below them,
the small hooded attic windows.

designed by Gaudí for the staircase that brings to mind the oversized backbone – perhaps of a dinosaur – a motif repeated on the ridge of the roof. In this respect, Gaudí had already reached the pinnacle of his achievements. It is difficult to say why he nevertheless took on the job that his friend Pere Milà offered. Perhaps it was the dimensions involved that tickled his fancy. At long last he did not need to create an illusion of largeness for a building, but was able from the very outset to build on a grand scale. The building was sited only a few houses away from the Casa Batlló, on the corner of the Paseo de Gracia and the Calle de Provenza. Gaudí had to depart from the structure he had adopted in earlier buildings as he now had to work with a corner-house. Previously he had emphasised the entranceway, either by means of a balcony-platform as in the Güell Palace, or a richly decorated oriel as in the Casa Calvet or the linking of balcony-platform and an archway in the Casa Batlló. Needless to say, in the Casa Milà, which was to serve as a large apartment block, several entranceways were required. To be precise, these are two residential buildings standing side by side, each with its own large gateway. Indeed, Gaudí originally planned a wide ramp for one of the two large courtyards so that even coaches could drive right up to the door; he later deviated from this plan however. Instead, he constructed an exit down below in an underground parking garage.

The surface area, over 10,000 square feet in size, posed a challenge. With a special design for the corner façade Gaudí gave the house the character of a detached building, although it was flanked by the rows of houses on the two streets. He softened the corner until it almost disappeared completely, and the building therefore seems more round than rectangular. Thus, strictly speaking, the house arches across the two

LEFT · The crest at the top of the stairwell is adorned with fragments of white marble.

FOLLOWING SPREAD · A group of chimneys.

streets. Gaudí took up the idea of a rotunda, an oversized tower, in designing two of the courtyards, which had to be large to provide enough light in the building. Here, again, he was treading virgin territory. Almost every one of his projects involved some such innovation, which usually, although with some delay, found its way into Barcelona's architecture. In the Casa Milà, Gaudí replaced the usual square patios with round courtyards that grew outwards as they moved upwards. Aerial views of the building give the impression that these inner courtyards suck everything magically towards them, not just air and light: they are enormous funnels. The slanting walls at the end of these shafts enabled Gaudí, as if merely in passing, to provide excellent lighting even for the attic. All these ideas are not ornamental in nature but rather serve utterly practical goals. This is another difference between the Casa Milà and the Casa Batlló. The Casa Milà is important not least because one can perceive in it a synthesis of Gaudí's late stylistic elements. And it is almost a matter of course that this synthesis involved Gaudí in a number of tussles with the municipal building authorities.

As in the Casa Batlló, a column in the façade juts out over the pavement by a full three feet. There was no question of removing it. The city wanted to permit the columns, but only if the projecting part of them was dispensed with. In an apparently quite conciliatory mood, Gaudí agreed, although on the condition that he be allowed to erect a plaque at the site stating the reasons why the columns had been thus mutilated – upon which the city withdrew its objections. The second confrontation with the authorities occurred when Gaudí once again exceeded the maximum height permitted. This was entirely predictable because Gaudí made a habit of continually changing his buildings in the course

LA PEDRERA

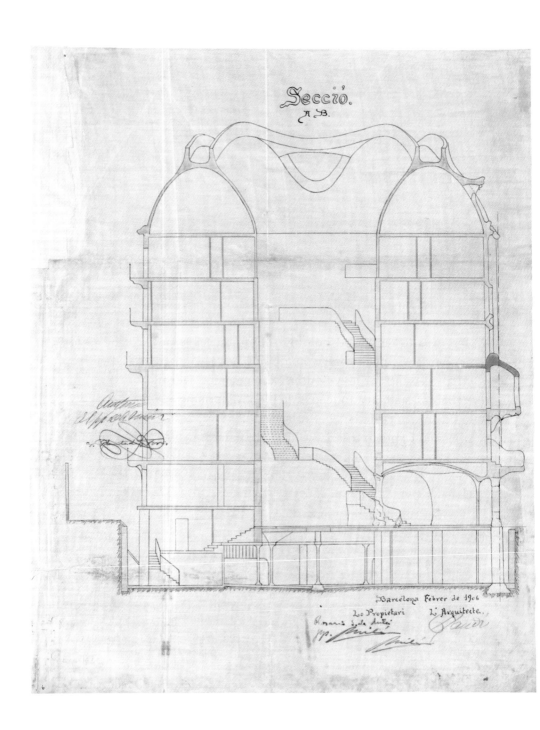

LA PEDRERA

of their construction. Here again Gaudí emerged victorious: the attic he had planned was installed.

Something that happened during construction work, however, caused Gaudí to lose interest in the building; he left it unfinished, although all that remained to be done was detailed finishing touches. Gaudí had planned to mount a series of dedications to the Virgin Mary on the façade. Indeed, he had designed a niche in which a haloed figure of Mary was to be placed holding the infant Jesus in her arms, surrounded by two angels, one worshipping her, the other, armed with a sword, protecting the holy figures from enemies. During construction work there was a hefty, indeed even bloody, uprising against the clergy in Barcelona. In the course of this "Semana Trágica" (26–30 July 1909), countless convents in the city went up in flames. In view of the anti-religious groundswell among the population, the owner of the building (and even his religious wife) judged it inappropriate to adorn the building with a series of religious representations and allusions – especially considering that it had already caused a stir. On this issue, Gaudí was not able to gain acceptance for his views, and the relationship between him and the owner was noticeably cooler thereafter.

Perhaps it was, after all, a good thing that Gaudí, who had become quite religious in the meantime and incorporated an increasing number of religious symbols in his buildings, did not integrate such elements in the Casa Milà as would have fitted better in the Sagrada Familia. In the absence of these sculptures, the outer façade of the building – as revolutionary as it may appear – seems to have been cast from one mould, though not with the "sugar icing" which is so typical of the Casa Batlló. Gaudí restricted himself to undressed stone to cover the outer walls –

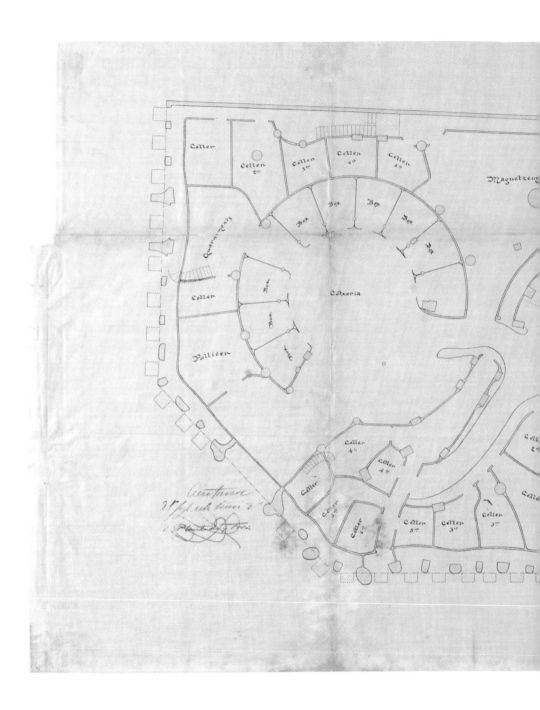

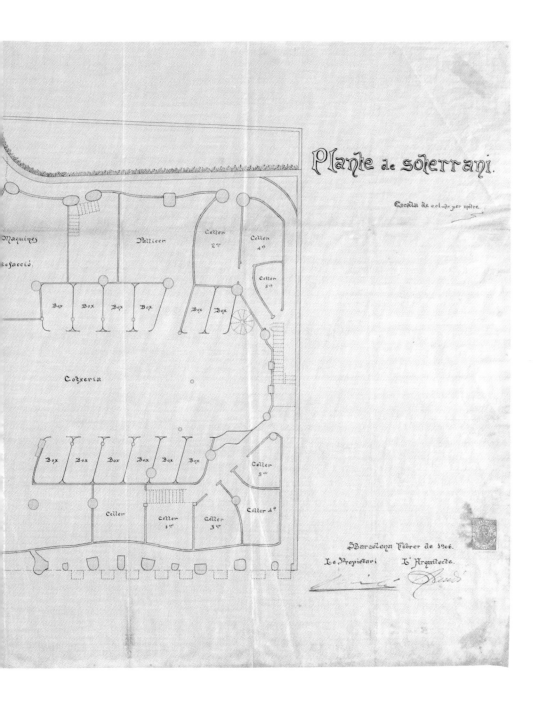

Floor plan of the basement.

PREVIOUS SPREAD · The ceiling painting is similarly positioned at both entrances, in this case the one leading from the small inner patio.

RIGHT · The entrance to the larger of the two patios is situated on Calle de Provenza.

FOLLOWING SPREAD · View from the staircase of the large entrance gate, which was designed by Gaudí himself.

the surface seems to follow no clear plan. Continually changing waves, bulges and niches create the overall impression of something asymmetrical, something "natural". This impression prompted observers and critics to draw all sorts of comparisons, which, however, all miss their mark. The house was called "La Pedrera" colloquially, i.e. "the quarry". Yet it is really only the colour and the surface that might be vaguely reminiscent of a quarry. Viewed from above, the house almost seems like the waves of the sea; yet, the line of waves is too smooth and harmonious for such an association. The Casa Milà is truly incomparable, and can be compared at most with Gaudí's own works. One might, for example, recollect the long, writhing bench in Güell Park, or the line of waves that tops the Casa Milà's roof and which also takes up the lines of the floors below.

Nothing about this house is uniform. The plans of each floor do not resemble one another. Gaudí was only able to create such a highly varied spatial structure because, as was hinted at in earlier projects, he mostly dispensed with carrying walls. There is not one to be found in the whole Casa Milà complex. Everything is borne by numerous pillars and supports. The rooms are of differing heights in keeping with the wavy form of the façade.

The whole building is less a house and more an enormous sculpture that seems to have been moulded by hand from soft plasticine. Rather than comparing it with nature, one does more justice to the house if one refers to a series of formal associations, for Gaudí was, above all, fascinated by plastic forms. "The forms in this unusual house seem to have been thrust, stretched and forged outwards from the innermost centre of it and then welded into unity. The outside and the inside, the concave and the convex, the whole and the individual parts, the walls and the

LA PEDRERA

LA PEDRERA

LEFT · An abstract ceiling painting above the staircase leading from the smaller patio to the second floor.

FOLLOWING SPREAD · Photo of historical home furnishings in the Casa Milà.

roof are all one undivided whole, pulsating with the same rhythm. What is usually termed a façade becomes a wide, wavy space in vertical terms; it becomes an indented whole where otherwise a window would be. And in horizontal terms, what had until modern times been regarded as a roof becomes a moving landscape." (Josef Wiedemann)

The harmony and yet variety of the façade corresponds to the design of the interior. There are no straight lines inside: everything appears to have been modelled and seems plastic. In the bulges and rounded cavities there is a continuous alternation of light and darkness, as if the light was performing some kind of dance. In this house one continually comes across new surprises. Even strict reminiscences of the Colegio Teresiano in the attic apartments, which are supported by white arching walls, fit in perfectly with the house. The roof sports a humorous landscape of almost surrealist sculptures that are in fact chimneys and air ducts. These are works of art that were only to be repeated at a later date in art history – but in sculpture, not in architecture, so that Gaudí's Casa Milà remained unique.

Above all, the house remained misunderstood for many years, and almost inevitably numerous parodies sprang up. But this also shows that, for all the ridicule that the building had to put up with, it nevertheless exercised a certain fascination over the public of its time – a fascination that was based unfortunately only on its external details. What was completely forgotten was that Gaudí's design for the Casa Milà was, as ever, based on practical considerations that were path-breaking; an example would be his forerunner of the underground garage in the basement.

ABOVE · Jujol's free-flowing waves on the ceiling are among the few surviving features of the original interior décor.

RIGHT · Attic story of one of the apartments, which Francisco Juan Barba Corsini furnished some time around 1956. During the 1993 renovation work, the attic was restored to its original state.

SAGRADA FAMILIA

Calle de Mallorca, Barcelona

If piles of stones, scaffolding and huge cranes were not part of the everyday furnishings of the church, one would be tempted to go to the main portal and enter this House of God. From the east the mighty building appears to be complete – a church in the Gothic tradition and yet completely a typical piece of 20th-century architecture, and indeed one that has taken a whole century to build. In 1883 Gaudí took over the management of the site; now, after many years of inactivity, completion is scheduled for 2026. When the church is finished, it will burst all dimensions asunder, and the first service will ring out like the choirs of Heaven: there is room for 1,500 singers, 700 children and 7 organs on the choir galleries. But for the moment, such a goal still seems to be a long way off.

PAGE 405 · The Nativity façade was already complete by 1932. The portal's soaring tympanum is topped by a Tree of Life. In a niche immediately below is a pelican, representing self-sacrifice and charity.

PREVIOUS SPREAD · Work in progress in 1905.

RIGHT · View of the interior of the Nativity façade as it was in 1927, not long after Gaudí's death. The towers are now almost finished.

It is probably impossible to find a church building anything like it in the entire history of art. One can normally speak of an artist's crowning achievement, often their last project but in Gaudí's case one cannot. His main opus is at the same time his life's work. Gaudí was engaged on the Sagrada Familia throughout his life. Yet no one would have anticipated such a lengthy process, least of all Gaudí when, in 1883, at the age of 31, he began to direct the construction work. For a long time he seems to have been filled with optimistic hopes with respect to the project's completion. In 1886 he still believed that he would complete the Sagrada Familia in as little as ten years as long as he was given a sum of 360,000 pesetas per year. Financial support was by no means guaranteed, for the church had been planned as a church of atonement, and the intention was to fund it entirely on the basis of donations. This led to considerable delays in construction work during the First World War: Gaudí went from house to house in person collecting funds.

The fact that in 1906 the church was still far from complete – work had got as far as the middle of one of the three (!) main façades – also had much to do with Gaudí's style of building. When he took on the role of directing he had a predominantly professional interest in the task. It was his first major construction project; he had been interested in church architecture for quite a while, but at the time he was fairly sceptical emotionally with regard to the Church. And scepticism was what he felt when studying the plans Villars had already drawn up. He could not and would not continue in the vein of the latter's neo-Gothic approach. However, the digging of the crypt – over which the apse was then to be erected – had already been completed; the columns in the crypt had indeed already reached some height. Gaudí would of course have much preferred to give

ABOVE · Gaudí's collaborator Joan Rubió i Bellver drew this view of the eastern façade of the Sagrada Familia, probably before 1905.

RIGHT · The Neo-Gothic façade connects to the Apostles' bell towers on the western façade.

SAGRADA FAMILIA

ABOVE · Wrought-iron cross above the entrance to the Nativity façade.

RIGHT · Spires of two Apostles' Towers.

LEFT AND ABOVE · The Passion Façade represents the final weeks in the life of Christ. Gaudí produced the drawing in 1911, at a time when he was deeply depressed state and had no wish to begin construction. Among the sculptures executed by Subirachs, in the middle of the bottom row seen in the picture, the figure on the left next to the soldier is believed to represent Gaudí himself.

BELOW · Ground plan of the church according to Gaudí's final design, published in 1929. The Latin cross is enclosed on three sides by a colonnade. Like the Gothic Chartres Cathedral, the drawing allows for three large portals.

RIGHT · Subirachs set his depiction of the Ascension of Christ on the bridge connecting to the Apostles' Towers in the centre of the western side of the church.

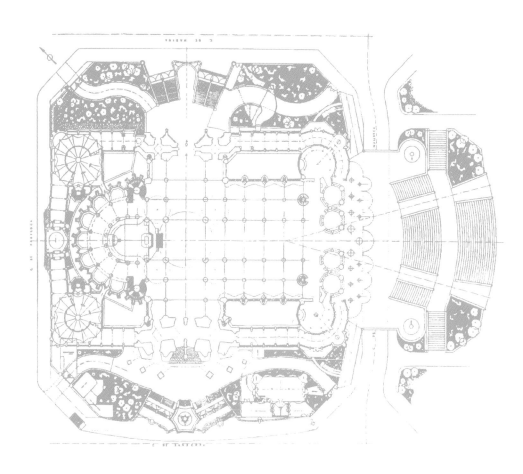

LEFT · Two soldiers controlling those on the Way of the Cross, by Josep Maria Subirachs, the artist who created the sculptures on the Passion Façade.

ABOVE · *Pilate washed his hands*, part of the group of figures depicting Jesus before Pilate.

the building a completely new direction, but he was obliged to work with what had already been achieved. And Villars' columns far from pleased him. Yet he held himself in check with regard to alterations. Admittedly, for a time he contemplated adding his own columns to those by Villars which were already there, but then realised that this would just lead to a nonsensical "civil war among the columns". The crypt as a consequence only bears Gaudí's trademarks to a limited extent. Nevertheless, he expanded Villars' porthole-like windows and moved the arches higher, so that the room received much more light and was not as oppressive as it had been in Villars' plan.

Gaudí's real achievements start with the apse over the crypt. Although the Gothic tradition remained a valid source of inspiration, Gaudí cleansed it of all superfluous forms. While retaining the Gothic window, he loosened its formal stringency by counterbalancing different circular elements to it. Seven chapels fan out from the altar, which is, by this very act, already in the visual centre of the building. What is more, the altar is free of all the overflowing ornamentation – typical for centuries – that tends to almost smother the altars of so many churches. This already demonstrates just how carefully Gaudí bore the religious functions of the church in mind. During his work on the Sagrada Familia he studied not only the ecclesiastical form of architecture, but also, and repeatedly, the liturgy of church services.

Yet the reason why the work was delayed so much was not only because Gaudí had to take over from another architect, but rather Gaudí's own approach. Instead of following a pre-determined plan, he preferred to evolve the project during the actual construction work. No other building bears better testimony to this method than the Sagrada Familia. It is

noteworthy that his first drawings for construction work say little about
the construction itself. At most they convey a general impression of the
building complex as planned, i.e. they are more or less atmospheric
portraits. An example of Gaudí's ever-changing mode of construction,
following ever new insights, is the design or rather the development of
the towers, the symbol of the church – if not landmark for Barcelona
as a whole. The overall model envisaged 12 bell towers, four for each of
the three main façades. Gaudí started them as rectangular towers; they
serve to frame the three respective portals that adorn each façade. It
then emerged that the column-like towers would protrude quite sharply
above the portals. Gaudí did not like this and therefore decided to make
them round, with fascinating results.

Although the towers taper towards the top, they have nothing in
common with the traditional, sharply pointed Gothic spires. Instead
Gaudí resorted to a formal innovation he had already used successfully
in the Colegio Teresiano. He designed the towers as rotational parabo-
las. The structure of the façade thus thrusts upward to quite a height.
The sharply pointed portals create a similar impression as in Gothic
cathedrals, although – like the apse windows – the sharpness of their
appearance is softened by the incorporation of circular elements; and
the rows of windows that lead up the towers as if in a spiral almost
wrench the observer along with them. The upward thrust of the towers
is, however, lessened by their rounded tops. Furthermore, Gaudí placed
a crowning boss on each tower, ending all upward movement. Viewed
from afar, these bosses have the appearance of enormous bishop's mi-
tres. Indeed, Gaudí wanted to allude to the further history of Christian-
ity – each tower is dedicated to one of the Apostles. Just as the Apostles

LEFT · Spires of the Apostles' Towers.

ABOVE · The cross-shaped endings of the canopies above the Apostle figures appear immediately in front of the windows on the way up.

turned into bishops, so too do the 12 towers each turn into a sort of mitre, and the whole tower seems to be an episcopal shepherd's crook.

This shows a typical feature of the Sagrada Familia. While the portals and towers initially seem to be designed purely in terms of architecture – full of imagination, but meaningful in terms of civil engineering – each of the church's different elements also has a second, symbolic function that was of even greater importance to Gaudí. There is nothing surprising about Bible scenes being used as "illustrations" on cathedrals. The Sagrada Familia has its share of them – indeed such a wealth can be encountered almost nowhere else. Gaudí did not just want to build a House of God, a place of worship; he conceived of the church as a catechism in stone, an oversized "book" in which the observer could read. This can be seen in the recurrent tendency to use symbols. The 12 towers, given their traditionality, are but a poor example. Yet they point to a central underlying structural characteristic. Gaudí imagined the church as the mystical Body of Christ. The centre is Christ himself, represented inside by the altar. Christ is, above all, the head of this body – as is symbolised by the cathedral's main spire, which is crowned with a great cross and alludes to Christ as the Saviour of mankind. The 12 towers that rise above the façades like crowns correspond to Christendom as a whole, represented by the Twelve Apostles.

All of this clearly has to be supplemented by one's imagination. Gaudí himself was not even able to witness the final completion of the main apse. The eastern façade, with which he started the main building, also remained incomplete. At the time of Gaudí's death only three of the four eastern towers had been finished. Of the three façades planned, he himself almost completed only the eastern one. The rest exists merely as

The Japanese sculptor Etsuro
Sotoo created the four large doors
of the Nativity façade with cheerful
and peaceful depictions of nature.

a plan and a plaster model (which, however, was destroyed by fire during the Spanish Civil War, and had to be reconstructed). Yet it is precisely the design of the façades that bears the imprint of Gaudí's conception. Each of the façades is dedicated to one aspect of Christ's ministry. By means of realistic and symbolic presentation and allusions, Christ appears as a human on earth, as the Saviour of mankind and as the judge over life and death on the Day of Judgment. Gaudí himself, however, was only able to portray Christ's life on earth. And there are thematic reasons why he started work on the eastern façade, the "Christmas façade". Friends and advisors had wanted him to start work on the western façade first, which would have attracted the inhabitants' attention more than the eastern, which faced away from the city (at that time). The western wall was, however, devoted to the sufferings of Christ in Gaudí's plans. It was Gaudí's opinion that to start with it might have frightened people away. And he was probably right. In keeping with the somewhat sad, pessimistic theme of the façade, it lacks all ornamentational decoration, and is dominated by crass and ugly forms. In contrast, with reference to Christ's life, Gaudí was able to choose more readily understandable forms of portrayal. Gaudí instilled the Flight to Egypt with hopes for the future. John the Baptist and his prophecy, and Jesus, showing the scribes what the true meaning of the words are – all this is portrayed simply and almost naively in numerous niches, almost as if presented as a Nativity play. This is reinforced by the names of the three portals. At the centre there is the Portal of Love, the largest of the three, depicting the birth of Christ and including a pelican as a symbol of love. It is flanked on the left by the Portal of Hope, which also portrays the two cruel events in Christ's childhood, namely Herod's murder of the children and the Flight to Egypt.

Finally, there is the Portal of Faith to the right of the main gate – with corresponding scenes from the Bible such as the Revelation of St John the Divine. There is a symbolic reason for these optimistic motives being carved into the eastern façade. "Ex oriente lux" – light comes from the east, and with it salvation, whereas the sufferings of Christ are depicted on the opposite western side, where the sun goes down. Light, which plays such an important role in Gaudí's secular buildings, is used here predominantly in a symbolic manner. This is true both of the compass direction of the main portal and of the use of lighting. The main tower as Gaudí planned it, soaring up above all else and symbolising Christ, was to be lit up by spotlights from the twelve "towers of the Apostles". At the same time, it was Gaudí's intention to beam strong light from the cross – in which the tower was meant to end – over the city, to light up the people and thus to illustrate Christ's words: "I am the light."

Colours were also used symbolically. Gaudí intended, for example, to use green for the Portal of Hope. With its rather more joyful themes, the eastern façade as a whole was meant to be bright and colourful, whereas Gaudí wanted to have the façade of Suffering in sombre colours. He certainly did not want to leave the stone in its natural hues. Gaudí hated monotony of colour – he found it unnatural. Nature, he frequently preached, never showed itself monochromatically or in complete uni-formity of colour, for it always contained a more or less clear contrast of colours. For Gaudí, who in the course of his life felt increasingly influ-enced by Mother Nature as a teacher, this meant that the architect was called upon to give all the elements of architecture at least some touch of colour. This colour design, however, remained at least for the time being a pipe dream, as did the façade which was probably intended as the most

ABOVE · The workshop in the basement of the Sagrada Familia in 1904. At the time, Gaudí was working on the design of the Apostles' Towers. A balcony rail for Casa Batlló can be seen on the left.

RIGHT · The model workshop in August 1917. By then, only models of the basilica could be seen here, but on this occasion there is also a model of the Nativity façade in the background.

Gaudí's drawing board in the former workshop next to the basilica.
Hanging from the ceiling are life-
sized models of animal figures for
the pillars in the apse. On the wall
on the right are St George and the
dragon, the same as they appeared
above the entrance to der Casa
Fernández y Andrés – otherwise
known as Casa Botines – in León.

Above the modest altar, the Crucified Christ hangs beneath a baldachin adorned with bunches of grapes and ears of wheat. The terracotta figure was designed by Francesc Fajula.

important one, i.e. the southern façade. It was supposed to be a special witness to the Glory of God, and a wide staircase was to lead up to it. The themes were to be Death and Hell, the Fall from Grace, the hard work of everyday life that resulted from this and, finally, the Creed as a statement of faith and therefore the first step towards salvation. The Creed, as so often in Gaudí's work, is depicted not in pictorial terms, but in the form of letters. It was to flare up between the bell towers in glowing letters. This method was used in the parts of the church that were completed last: on the eastern façade "Sanctus, Sanctus, Sanctus" can be read in the middle of the spiralling openings of the bell towers, directing one's eyes upwards – almost like a joyful cheer at the ascent into Heaven. Gaudí had always liked integrating letters, indeed even complete words, into his buildings, Güell Park showing the most instances. In the Sagrada Familia, the letters usually have a symbolic function, and they are intended to point repeatedly to the essential messages conveyed by the church building, which is more than the House of God: it is, in reality, a work of art shaped not unlike a sculpture. Often we do not know where one sculpture starts and the other finishes. Using a technique similar to that adopted in the Casa Milà, the façade of the Sagrada Familia is built mainly of material other than stone, and we get the impression that the sculpture consists of numerous ornaments moulded out of soft material – clay or wax – which then frame or cover the biblical scenes. The letters lend emphasis to the messages conveyed by the scenes. One encounters anagrams, for example, of Jesus, Mary and Joseph in the windows of the apse. In contrast to most biblical portrayals, Joseph is given a very predominant position here. This is understandable, given that the church was built at the instigation of the "Association of Worshippers of

**RIGHT AND FOLLOWING
SPREAD** · A brightly-coloured
stained-glass window.

St Joseph". The main chapel in the crypt is dedicated to him, and an ef-
figy is to be found on the main portal of the eastern façade. The frequent
depiction of a bee can be taken as a symbol of the industriousness of the
worker. Yet there are even clearer signs of the status to which Joseph has
been raised in this church. There are repeated portrayals of his tools. A
large statue shows Jesus exercising his "foster-father's" profession – with
a chisel in one hand. In Gaudí's presentation of the scene where Mary
and Joseph search for their son, who is sitting with the scribes in the syn-
agogue, it is Joseph who leads the way – unlike the usual depictions in
which Mary leads the search. And, finally, Joseph is portrayed as guardian of the church: as the helmsman, he steers the ship (the church) safely
past all dangers.

In the face of this wealth of symbolic allusions, which fuse the
church – at least its façades – into a "picture" with expressive power,
one might be tempted to forget Gaudí, the great master builder. The
abundant ornamentation of the eastern façade slightly deceives us into
overlooking the fact that, with the Sagrada Familia, Gaudí succeeded
in creating an imposing piece of architecture. It shows his roots in tradition, although his personal style is forever in evidence. The floorplan
follows that of the main examples of Gothic cathedrals: the Sagrada
Familia was conceived of as a basilica with five naves, and a transept
with three aisles (the three portals in the eastern and western façades
respectively are the entrances to the transept's three aisles). The floorplan thus has the shape of a cross. The main nave, including the apse,
was to be 311 feet long, the transept 196 feet. This corresponds largely
with the shape of Cologne Cathedral (which Gaudí on the whole viewed
positively). With such dimensions, however, it is obvious that there are

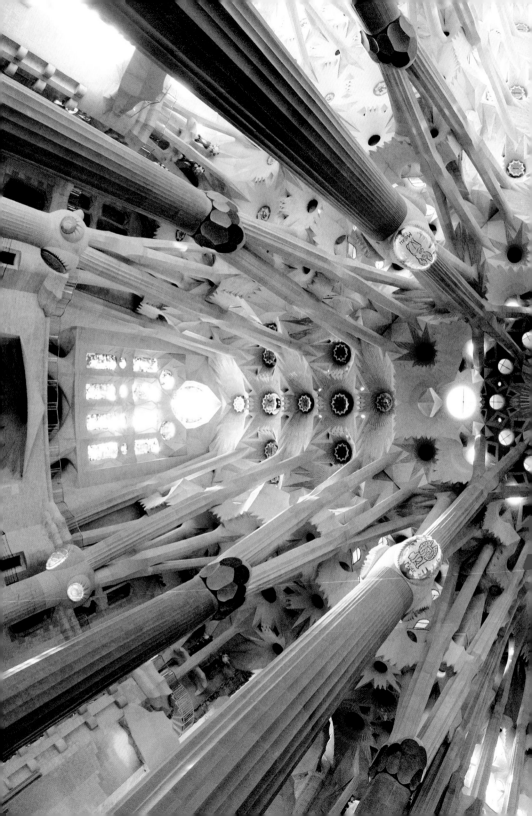

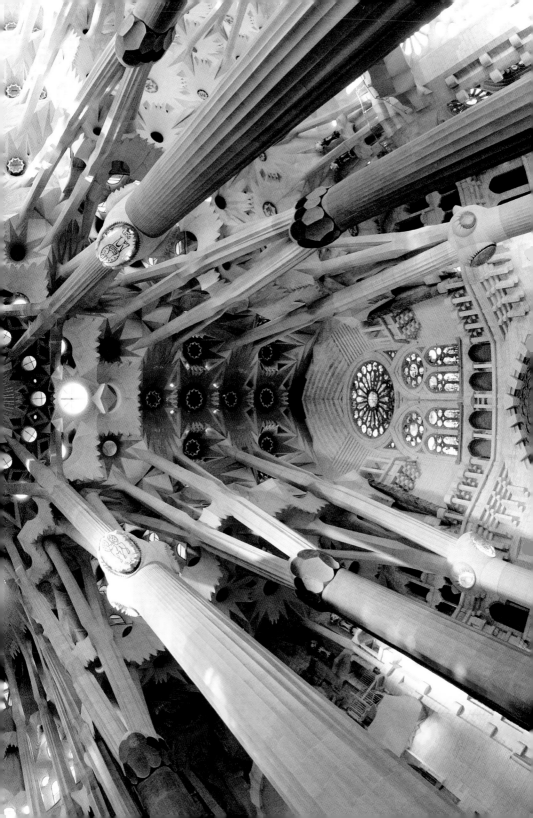

PREVIOUS SPREAD · The view from below of the ceiling above the nave clearly shows how the columns decorated with grooves each branch out so that each can help to provide support for the ceiling.

LEFT · Above where the nave and side aisles cross, back-lit glass medallions portraying the Four Evangelists are inset into the support structure.

FOLLOWING SPREAD · The ceiling dissolves into numerous radiant openings, reminiscent of flowers.

problems of civil engineering. Cologne Cathedral has enormous columns and flying buttresses – the "crutches" Gaudí condemned Gothic architecture for having used. He manages without these aids. The Sagrada Familia is the best example of Gaudí's fundamental discovery that an interlinking of parabolic arches and slanting columns can bear the hefty weight of even large vaulting masonry. He had already proved this on a small scale in the Colegio Teresiano and the riding hall on the Güell estate, in fact even in his first project, the factory halls of Mataró. In the Sagrada Familia he combined this construction principle with the insights he had gained from studying nature. With regard to load-bearing capacity, he took the eucalyptus tree as his example. It thus comes as no surprise that the network of columns in the main nave of the Sagrada Familia resembles a forest of stone. One gets the impression that the slanting columns cannot actually bear the weight from above; yet, Gaudí's buildings have always proved to be durable. The degree to which his successors bungled the work on the Bishop's Palace in Astorga shows just how precarious it can be to deviate from Gaudí's constructions, carefully rehearsed and tested beforehand by means of models. His unique construction of columns has a surprising side effect. The aisles of the church appear ethereally light. The columns seem to bear no weight. Gaudí said that in his work the classical contrast in architecture between burdening and bearing was overcome in a positive sense. A column in the eastern façade illustrates this theory: Gaudí took as the base of the pillar two giant stone tortoises. The columns seem to grow up out of the carapaces, in other words to sprout upwards although they should really crush the animals. One seldom finds so graphic a realisation of theory.

The fanned-out, funnel-
shaped crown mouldings owe
much to Catalan brick-built vaults.

Gaudí's achievements as a building constructor also give cause for
scepticism. There is hardly another architect who concerned himself so
much with all the different tasks that arise on a building site. In fact,
in the last years of his life, Gaudí lived in his small workshop on the
site. He was to be encountered everywhere, devoting attention to the
smallest of engineering problems. And he was just as clear about how to
solve them as he was on the large-scale constructional problems. He left
behind him models that showed how he conceived the finished church
to look, but it is questionable whether it can ever be completed without
him. Even César Martinell i Brunet, a friend of Gaudí's, had a sceptical,
if humorous, opinion of the problem. He stated that the church should
be regarded as completed and that this was more than just an optimistic approach considering that Gaudí had not finished a single façade. In
fact, he maintained that their completion was still a very long way off.

He was not exaggerating. Indeed, the continuation of Gaudí's projects after his death would seem to prove the point. The eastern façade
is admittedly now complete, but it is still far too early to speak of the
building as a church. The western façade has meanwhile started to take
shape – and Gaudí's plans and models have been followed carefully. But
work on it has taken up the last three decades: again and again one hears
of yet another small portion being inaugurated. This might lead us to
question whether work on the church should be continued at all. There
were critics of the church even in Gaudí's day, but, with his vision of the
building ever before his eyes, he was able to prevail in person. Nowadays, this persistence has to exist without Gaudí's dynamism to push
it ahead. Not only the immense costs would speak against continuing
construction efforts (by 1914, the project had already run into more than

three million pesetas and Gaudí was still in the middle of it), but also the fact that there are plenty of uncompleted Gaudí buildings. Indeed, it is almost a trademark of his that he did not finish his buildings. Yet this must be balanced against Gaudí's statement that the Sagrada Familia was the first in a series of utterly new cathedrals. And that places an obligation on us – as does the fact that the Sagrada Familia has long since become the landmark of Barcelona. Even at a time when the first bell towers were still in their infancy, gradually taking on shape and stature, the inhabitants of the city already identified with "their" church. After all, the bell towers soar above the city (the two middle towers are both over 300 feet high; the main tower was planned to reach 557 feet). And finally, with this project Gaudí had rooted himself firmly in the grand tradition of mediaeval cathedral building. These were also not the work of one architect – but of whole generations. Gaudí has truly left his city a magnificent legacy, even if it is not without its problems. Throughout his entire working life, Gaudí was in search of an architecture capable of successfully combining the spiritual with the functional. In so doing, he had to acknowledge two things that needed to be considered. Firstly, the design process was far from over with the production of a drawing. Secondly, the key to a successful piece of architecture did not lie in the ornamentation of the façades or the interior decor, but in the sense of space generated by the structure itself. On the one hand, this meant that even when construction was underway, he would forever be making changes and, having visited the site and checking the original measurements, would make significant adjustments to the initial plans. Even after, in the interests of safety, constructing an elaborate model construction, Gaudí was never beyond making startling changes of direction. On the

other hand, he had complete confidence in the creative contributions of artists, artisans and other architects and was happy to grant them extensive autonomy, although their work was always subject to his final approval. Hence, it is well-nigh impossible to imagine what results Gaudí himself would have achieved had he been able to complete the Sagrada Familia, since the turning point in his work came when his religious conviction became the raison d'être of his architecture.

As early as 1965, an open letter, signed by almost all Spain's leading architects and many of their European colleagues, vigorously cast doubt on the wisdom of continuing to build the cathedral. It was neither beneficial to the urban community nor to the propagation of religious belief and most certainly not of any value from the point of view of maintaining the integrity of Gaudí's work, to resume construction.

Increasing public interest in Gaudí's oeuvre and restoration carried out on the famous site in no way helped to reduce the problem. On 2008, a further manifesto, signed by influential representatives of cultural life, stated that restoration work and use by tourists was causing considerable damage to virtually every one of Gaudí's best-known buildings. There is heavy criticism of events at the Sagrada Familia: "Today, neither we, nor anyone else knows where the architect's work begins and ends. What stands out is the mediocrity of a group of technicians and developers, who are well-meaning but full of an anachronistic paternalism in the best of cases, and are once again using Gaudí to make their personal mark on the building to the detriment of the original work." As Oscar Tusquets Blanca pointed out, the problem is not only the architecture but Gaudí's basic idea of using sculptures to present the building's façades as visual narratives. Indeed, Subirach's work on the Passion Façade despite, or

RIGHT · Paths also lead through the building on higher levels. Here they feature colourful light, which comes partially from exterior light shining through the stained-glass windows and partially from artificial interior lighting.

FOLLOWING SPREAD · Gaudí planned to dedicate each of the 56 columns to one Sunday in the annual liturgical calendar.

maybe even because of, his attempt to produce a modern interpretation, seems ineffectual compared to Gaudí's Nativity façade, while the failure of the main Glory Façade seems to be inevitable. Manuel Borja-Villel, the influential director of Madrid's Museo Nacional Centro de Arte Reina Sofía (MNCARS), commented: "What they are constructing has little to do with the spirit of Gaudí. It has more to do with building a tourist attraction and for propaganda purposes." Anyone visiting the church in 2020 will be alarmed at how the cathedral building site – along with other examples of Gaudí's architecture – has now become the destination of thousands of tourists, stuck on a conveyor belt-like circuit around the city sights. Many of them see every surface bearing the "Gaudí" brand name as the background to a short-lived selfie. In truth, little remains of the zeal with which Gaudí and the other initiators of the Sagrada Familia project pursued their goals. Sadly, it is an historical irony that the vast numbers of commentators who claim to be searching for the spiritual message in Gaudí's works simply destroy such a message, precisely because there are so many different theories. From a cathedral, designed to unite an urban community in Christian contemplation, the seeds of discord have sprouted and spread to a city that can no longer tolerate "overtourism", in a tragic perversion of its creator's vision.

SAGRADA FAMILIA SCHOOLS

Calle de Cerdeña, Barcelona

When Gaudí drafted a blueprint for a school to be built on the Sagrada Familia site for children of the craftspeople and other workers employed there, it was only intended as a provisional solution until construction of the church was completed. However, it was clear that the school would be designed to last and therefore it was worthwhile making it a solid brick-built structure. Gaudí himself believed it should stand out as a project to which much thought had been given, despite the fact that there was scarcely any money available to pay for this unpretentious, functional building. Decorative design was out of the question and certainly the school did not comply with the strict requirements usually associated with schools. Although the ground plan showed little room for manoeuvre on a site where space was restricted, there was sufficient to accommodate three classrooms.

PAGE 459 · The brilliant design, and especially the curvilinear roof of the Sagrada Familia School building, are is a delight to behold.

PREVIOUS SPREAD · By relocating the school building on the side, the former street side now faces the church.

RIGHT · Site plan with the school yards.

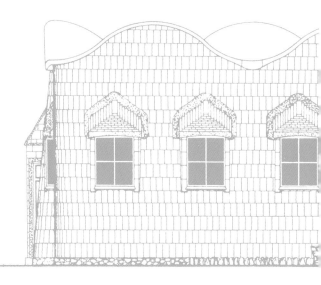

Nevertheless, Gaudí accomplished the feat of turning an obligatory task into a small work of art, one which is considered by many to be the best example of Gaudí's genius, which here, without embellishments, are plain to see.

It was also his reputation which prevented the school being demolished in 2006. As work on the church progressed, the school site was getting in the way and was about to be demolished altogether. Instead, with some modifications, it was allotted a new location. However, this was not the first time that the school had to be rebuilt. In 1936 during the Spanish Civil War the building was gutted by fire and the roof, which rested on a continuous girder along the central axis, caved in. The reconstruction survived only three years before suffering a similar fate. More major repairs took place in 1943. When work was completed, very little of Gaudí's school could be regarded as original. Even so, what still survived were the main ideas that characterised his work and which, even now, are strikingly original. The wave-like roof extends as far as the opposite sides of the building. Everything here appears to be in motion; even at ground level the walls begin in undulations, gradually straightening up as they expand upwards towards the roof. Anyone entering the building will see that behind the

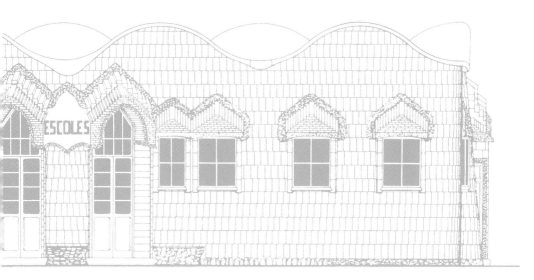

waves lies some very simple geometry, in the shape of the continuous straight girders supporting the roof. All this "free-form" architecture is deceptive, as this is a very simple construction following traditional building methods. Gaudí used the very simplest material, including his much-favoured clay bricks, with which he followed the Catalan style, laying them vertically in two rows to assemble the walls. The undulations of the roof make the façade more viable, likewise the sine-waved roof adds a certain degree of support. Le Corbusier was so impressed by the building that he immediately made a drawing. Because the two interior walls had no load-bearing function, the building was divided into three classrooms and, according to need, could easily be arranged differently. Gaudí even envisaged three areas of the courtyard becoming arranged as open-air classrooms. Functionality transforms this seemingly unprepossessing building into a small masterpiece.

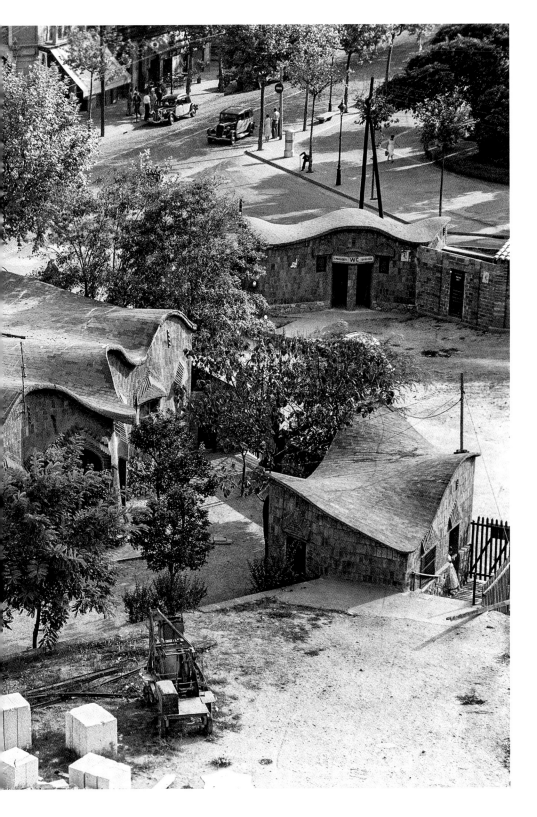

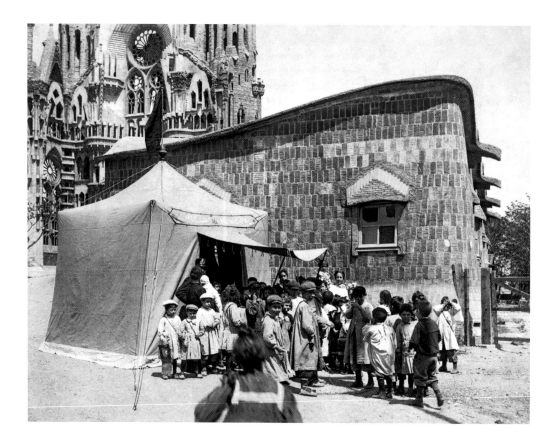

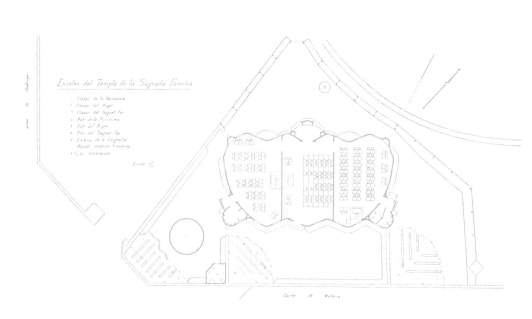

SAGRADA FAMILIA SCHOOLS

PREVIOUS SPREAD · Later, there were some additions to the main building where the classrooms were situated. Toilets were installed in small outbuildings along the outer walls.

LEFT ABOVE · In 1909, a vaccination program, sponsored by the city of Barcelona's health authorities, was put into operation in a tent in front of the school building.

LEFT BELOW · Site plan with the school yards.

BELOW · In this 1913 photograph of the classroom, it is easy to recognise the ceiling construction.

FOLLOWING SPREAD · In this photo, taken shortly after 1910, the work on the first Apostle Towers of the church is in full swing. The school building can be seen at the front right.

APPENDIX

THE
COMPLETE
WORKS

BIOGRAPHY

PHOTO CREDITS

BIBLIOGRAPHY

MAP

THE COMPLETE WORKS

CEMETERY GATE ILL. 01
1875 · Architectural School Project
While Gaudí was at architectural school he produced a sketch based on a perspective drawing of a cemetery gate. The classical simplicity of the architectural form is combined with a variety of artistic elements, some symbolic, others figurative, based on the Book of Revelation, the last book in the Bible. Flaming torches at the corners of the structure add a certain apocalyptic effect. In the opinion of the potential customer, this first draft consisted of too little architecture and too much drama. In any event, the design was never implemented.

COURTYARD FOR A PROVINCIAL GOVERNMENT HEADQUARTERS
1876 · Architectural School Project
As a second-year student at the school of architecture, Gaudí created this design for a provincial government building. The surviving documents include a cross-sectional drawing and a detailed 1:25 drawing of the balustrade and support structures of the atrium with its glass roof. Some remarkable features of the latter, which together produce the overall effect, include the brick-built arches, the ornamental stonework with riveted steel girders and pillars of unidentifiable materials. From the colours used, we might assume that the pillars are made of marble, but they could also be painted, circular columns of cast iron.

EMBARKATION PIER
1876 · Architectural School Project
This sketch of a pier for pleasure boats was intended as an entry in a drawing competition. Towering above a lakeside pier, the more or less rectangular structure has four rounded platforms at each corner, the two front ones connecting to a pavilion. Shade is provided by canvasses stretched over sloping struts set in the water. The two surviving colour sketches show two alternative architectural designs for the towers, viewed from the front and side. Apparently, Gaudí was exploring and comparing the effect of a neo-baroque construction with that of a neo-Gothic one.

MONASTERIO DE MONTSERRAT ILL. 02
1876—1877 · Restoration of the church
When the architect Francisco de Paula del Villar was commissioned to restore the Basilica of the Monastery of Montserrat, destroyed by French troops in 1812, he hired Antoni Gaudí, still a student, as a draughtsman. However, it was not a successful collaboration. Gaudí was unimpressed by the architect, from whom he later took over the construction of the Sagrada Familia. However, the client finally found his suggestions for the decoration of the church, especially the shrine of the Virgin Mary, too expensive.

FOUNTAIN IN PLAZA DE CATALUÑA
1877 · Architectural School Project
Yet another student project, this is the design for a monumental, 40-metre-high fountain in Barcelona's Plaza de Cataluña. This square marking the intersection between the Old Town and Eixample, where the Sarrià-Barcelona train station is situated, called for an imposing style. Gaudí's fountain is a round, multilevel structure with four pavilions standing in front. From the centre, like a water-borne rocket, shoots an octagonal crest, on which eight caryatids support the sky above them. Because of the

01

SECCION LONGITUDINAL
Y
CAMARIN
Escala de 1 por M.

02

03

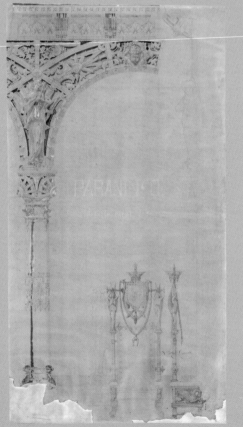

04

Tamaño natural   Barcelona 1878

05

later construction of the nearby Metro station, no monumental piece of architecture was ever erected on this site.

PARC DE LA CIUTADELLA ILL. 03

1877—1882 · Collaboration on several designs of the Parc de la Ciutadella

Josep Fontserè i Mestre, creator of the master plan for Barcelona's newly created city park, sought the help of Antoni Gaudí, still a student at the time, to produce designs. Since then, there has been a lively debate over which of the many individual features bear Gaudí's signature. Those most frequently mentioned include various balustrades, the two large entry gates each flanked by two sculptures on large pedestals and the grotto behind the waterfall, as well as the structural analysis of the reservoir feeding the cascade.

MAIN HALL FOR A UNIVERSITY ILL. 04

1877 · Architectural School Project

As his final project completed at the Escuela Provincial de Arquitectura in Barcelona, Gaudí presented the design for a large assembly hall for a university. Presumably, he had Barcelona's main university in mind. Gaudí represents the hall with its oval floorplan and overhead lighting, with classical fresco painting, thereby creating an idiosyncratic contrast to a certain Moorish influence in other parts of the structure. Gaudí would frequently and without hesitation borrow examples from architectural history and bring them quirkily together in his idiosyncratic way in order to create something surprising and altogether new. On this occasion his work was not sufficiently convincing and did not earn him good grade.

RELIQUARY ILL. 05

1878 · A private commission

A remarkably precise, full-scale, freehand drawing shows a small reliquary. It is unclear under what circumstances or for which commission the piece was designed, but is not unlikely that it was intended for Josep Maria Bocabella i Verdaguer, for whom Gaudí later created a private altar. Here, Gaudí's penchant for a combination of sculpture and metalwork is clear to see, as it is in his architecture.

DISPLAY CASE FOR ESTEVE COMELLA

1878 · Universal Exposition in Paris

The glovemaker Esteve Comella owned a luxury store on Barcelona's Calle de Aviñón and also appeared at the 1878 Universal Exposition in Paris. Gaudí designed an exhibition showcase for him, and had it built in Eudald Puntí i Gorchs's workshop. The showcase itself, together with its contents, was awarded a silver medal. It also marked a significant moment in Gaudí's career, since it led to his first meeting with Eusebi Güell, from whom he would later receive many important commissions.

GIROSSI KIOSKS

1878 · Street kiosks and restrooms

In the city of Barcelona's planning application archives, there is a plan entitled *Permission for Enrique Girossi to Situate Urinal Kiosks in Public Places*. The word *kiosk* often refers to a flower stall, but this could be a way of disguising its intended use. The floor plan for this wrought-iron construction with a beautifully decorated roof shows that ladies would enter the toilet cubicle from the left and gentlemen from the right, while at the rear of the building men could also access a public pissoir.

THEATRE MIRÓ

1878 · Enclosure wall and gate for Pablo Miró's theatre

A garden wall, a gate and a portico were part of one of Pablo Miró's construction projects in the Sant Gervasi district, developed in conjunction with a theatre. According to Joan Bassegoda i Nonell, part of it was completed but torn down again soon after.

OBRERA MATARONENSE
1878—1982 · Buildings for a workers' cooperative in Mataró
The socialist workers' cooperative, Obrera Mataronense, was planning an ambitious development, which would not only include factory buildings, but also a vocational training centre and a meeting room. One of the organisation's founders, Salvador Pagès, was a friend of Gaudí's and it was he who presented the young architect with his first major commission. The bleaching shed with its vaulted wooden roof, whose arches conform to the so-called catenary curve, still survives. For financial reasons, these arches were put together from many single beams, a process which, for all its simplicity, creates a sizeable, column-free space. Two residential buildings designed for workers no longer exist, while the bleaching shed is now an art museum.

COMILLAS CHAPEL
1878 · Furniture for the chapel in the Palacio de Comillas, Santander
Gaudí designed several pieces of furniture for the burial chapel of the Marquis of Comillas' family home, the Palacio Comillas in Santander, built by Joan Martorell. Some pieces in the neo-Gothic style still survive, among them the lectern in the picture and a chair in beautifully carved walnut, with red velvet upholstery.

PLAZA REAL LIGHTING
ILL. 06
1878 · Streetlamps for Barcelona
Commissioned by Barcelona City Council, Gaudí designed new gaslights as well as the corresponding installation plan. His design sets a wrought-iron lamp post on a stone plinth, decorated with four motifs. Each post supports six arms, accentuated by strips of brown, each bearing a lamp covered by a hemispherical shade in white glass, the light from which is reflected on the ground below.

The lamp posts on the Plaza Real are crowned by the winged helmet of the Roman god Mercury and a serpent. Smaller versions with three arms were erected on the Plaza del Palacio and the Paseo de Juan de Borbón.

WORK DESK
1878 · Furniture for his own workshop
Immediately after his graduation, Gaudí built a work desk for himself, based on his own sophisticated design. Instead of the usual flat surface placed on two pedestals, a massively heavy piece of cabinetmaking only rests on four legs. The two exposed storage spaces suspended either side serve add extra support, while a roll top provides a finishing touch to the desk. The lower half of the desk, built in Eudald Punti's workshop, is lavishly decorated with aquatic plants, birds, serpents and insects. It was destroyed by fire in the workshop in 1936.

GIBERT PHARMACY
1879 · Decoration for the Gibert Pharmacy in Barcelona
For Joan Gibert i Casals' pharmacy Gaudí designed the counter and built-in furniture, as well as the lettering and the shop front, the lower part of which was framed with marble, the upper part with wood. A Rod of Asclepius [the internationally recognised symbol of medicine] topped by a decorative shield, can be seen on either side of the door. The Arabic style of the marquetry lent the pharmacy an exotic feel, but also an air of respectability. The only surviving photograph also shows a suitably designed easy chair in which customers could relax.

ALLEGORICAL PAGEANT
1879 · Drawings for an allegorical pageant in Vallfogona de Riucorb
In 1879, the town of Vallfogona de Riucorb was preparing a pageant in honour of the poet Francesc Vicent Garcia i Torres, for which

07

08

09

Gaudí provided five drawings for floats and costumes. The date is surprising, since at that time no special celebration of the poet was due, and it may have been that plans were already under way in readiness for the 300th anniversary of his birth. Gaudí's five drawings dealt with the grain harvest, olive cultivation and vine growing, with participants carrying torches and donkeys adorned with flowers drawing the floats. However, the planned event never took place.

CONVENT OF JESUS, MARY AND JOSEPH ILL. 07

1879—1882 · Lamps and an altar at the Convent of Jesus, Mary and Joseph in Tarragona

The College of Jesus, Mary and Joseph was founded in 1877 by Father Josep Manyanet i Vives. Gaudí's niece was a pupil at the school and he was able to carry out some small works on the school building. He also designed an altar with a monstrance, lamps and a mosaic floor for the church constructed for the same congregation between 1876 and 1881. On the alabaster altar, two angels appear either side of a cylindrical case holding the monstrance. In 1909 the altar was destroyed, but in 1969 it was restored in somewhat different style by Joan Bassegoda i Nonell.

PASSEIG DE MAR ILL. 08

1880 · Lighting for the Passeig de Mar in Barcelona

Following his design of street lamps in two squares in the city centre, Gaudí received another commission to draw up plans for lighting along the new promenade along the harbour. Between 1878 and 1881, the old city wall reaching down into the water was demolished and the rubble transformed to create the Paseo de Colón. Gaudí worked alongside the engineer Josep Serramalera i Aleu. Together they designed a series of eight gigantic lamp posts resting on foundations running along the water's edge from Villanueva Station to

the *offshore* neighbourhood of Barceloneta, each one named after a Catalan admiral.

SAN SEBASTIÁN CASINO

1880—1881 · Competition entry for a Casino in San Sebastián

For the 1880 competition to design a new casino in San Sebastian, Gaudí submitted a plan, which sadly has not survived. He is thought to have included various ideas dating from his student days. When gambling became illegal in 1924, the building created by Luis Aladrén Mendivi and Adolfo Morales de los Ríos became the city's town hall.

CASA VICENS ILL. 09

1878—1888 · House in Calle de les Carolines, 18–24 in the Gràcia neighbourhood of Barcelona

As early as 1878 Gaudí completed a design for a summer residence for the industrialist Manuel Vicens in the small town of Gràcia, at the time not yet incorporated into the city. The project did not begin in earnest until 1883. The boundary of the narrow building was extended as far as that of a neighbouring convent so as to create space for a garden which on the other side would be closed off by an artificial waterfall. Later, the layout was drastically changed. In 1925, the new owner Antoni Jover commissioned the architect Joan Baptista Serra de Martínez to widen it to almost double the size. The waterfall was torn down in 1946.

HUNTING LODGE ILL. 10

1882 · Hunting lodge in Sitges

Eusebi Güell owned a plot of land in El Garraf, where he wanted to erect a hunting lodge to Gaudí's design. Gaudí's plan was never implemented but many of the features introduced were to reappear in his later buildings. What was striking was the extraordinarily detailed and painstaking drawings with which Gaudí presented the project. Some believe that the design showed similarities to Gaudí's unsuccessful entry to the San Sebastián competition. While he never directly used such drawings, he did demand the return of his plans on the grounds that he might need them for another potential assignment.

CHAPEL SANTO SACRAMENTO ILL. 11
1883 · Chapel for the parish church in Alella
Gaudí designed, in meticulous detail, an altar for a side chapel of the parish church in Alella. Within the framework of the church's Gothic architecture, he placed seven windows with seven angels blowing trumpets, a reference to the Book of Revelation. Bishop Jaume Català i Albosa approved the plans, but the work was never carried out. The only change Gaudí made to the lower regions of the church was a narrow staircase leading to the bell tower with the steps in triangular form so as to leave space on the ground floor.

SUMMER HOUSE
1881 · A temporary summer house in Comillas
To mark the visit of King Alfonso XII, Gaudí designed a small summer house on a raised platform with a fabric roof, also intended for the Marquis of Comillas to enjoy. After the royal visit the summer house was dismantled and later rebuilt on the land surrounding the Finca Güell in Barcelona.

FURNITURE
1884 · Furnishings for Casa Vicens in Alella
Between 1883 and 1888 Gaudí spent more time in the Casa Vicens in Alella, while he was building the new house in Gràcia for its owner Manuel Vicens. At this time, Gaudí was able to create some pieces of furniture for the property, such as a corner cabinet and a small open fireplace.

EL CAPRICHO ILL. 12
1883—1885 · Casa Díaz de Quijano in Comillas, Santander
Antonio López y López de Lamadrid, who in 1878 received the title Marquis of Comillas, had made his fortune from activities including slave trafficking in Cuba. He was responsible for the construction of a number of prestigious buildings in the city. His brother-in-law, Máximo Díaz de Quijano, commissioned Gaudí to build him a summer residence in the palace garden. Guided by earlier building plans, Gaudí based his design on the existing conservatory, his drawings showing a simple house whose decorative tiles and little turret with a wrought-iron balustrade made it seem more spectacular than it actually was.

FINCA GÜELL
1884—1887 · Gate and stables on Avenida de Pedralbes, 7 in Barcelona
One year after Eusebi Güell bought a large property in Les Corts de Sarrià, he commissioned Gaudí to construct the three entry gates. The main entrance on Avenida Pedralbes is famous for its wrought-iron Dragon Gate. The dragon, a frequent motif in Gaudí's work and usually a reference to St George, Catalonia's patron saint, is here depicted as Ladon, the mythological guardian of the Garden of the Hesperides. One of the two buildings on either side was the gatekeeper's lodge, the other a stable with 14 stalls and rooms for the riding school.

ALTAR
1885 · Altar for Casa Bocabella in Barcelona
The bookseller Josep María Bocabella, the driving force behind the building of the Sagrada Familia, had his own collection of relics and had also obtained permission to install a private altar in his house. Gaudí's design proposed a marble-clad alcove in a carved mahogany altar. However, the three images are only mounted prints. The altar was consecrated in 1890 and is still privately owned.

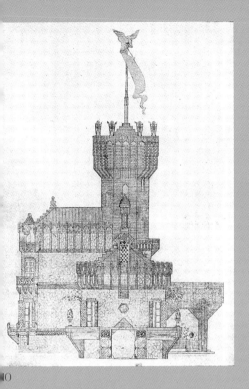

10

Progecto de Capilla del SS. Sacramento para la Iglesia Parroqual de S. Feliy de Alirelti.

11

12

THE COMPLETE WORKS　　　　　　　　**481**

SAGRADA FAMILIA

1883—1926 • Temple of the Sagrada Familia in Barcelona

In 1884 Gaudí was officially commissioned to continue the construction of the church started by Francisco Paula del Villar y Lozano, which began when the bookseller Josep María Bocabella experienced a religious awakening and donated a plot of land. In fact, Gaudí had already started work on the unfinished project the previous year. To the plans with which he was confronted for a neo-Gothic church with three aisles, he added two more naves. These were crossed by three transepts leading to the Nativity façade on the east side – the only part of the church to be completed in Gaudí's lifetime – and the west-facing Passion Façade. The most conspicuous deviations from the neo-Gothic canon are the 18 towers, each symbolising a biblical figure, with Christ represented by the tallest tower in the centre.

GÜELL PALACE

1885—1889 • Palace in Calle Nou de la Rambla, 3–5 in Barcelona

Güell's residence in Barcelona's old town was supposed to be built right next to his father's house, which meant that it would be situated on a relatively small plot of land. Between the two entrances, highlighted by parabolic arches, an allegorical bird carved in wrought iron sits enthroned, perching on a Catalan coat of arms, also in wrought iron. Visitors would be able to enter the courtyard in their carriages and their horses would be attended to in the basement. Güell's library and office were housed on a mezzanine while overhead a lavish suite of rooms provided the space required for important events. The building is crowned by an assortment of 20 differently designed chimneys and ventilation shafts.

EXHIBITION PAVILION ILL. 13

1888 • Addition to the Pavilion of the Compañía Trasatlántica in Barcelona

Claudio López Bru, son of Antonio López, gave Gaudí work relating to the 1888 Barcelona Universal Exposition pavilion of Companyia Transatlàntica (Compañía Trasatlántica Española), whose main business was passenger transport to the New World. Probably, Gaudí only provided some additional decorative details, since the pavilion had already been used for the 1887 National Maritime Exhibition in Cádiz. The entrance, modelled on the Court of the Lions in the Alhambra, and the wooden latticework protecting the side panels from the sun, might have reminded Gaudí of the crenellated turrets of the Alcazaba in Malaga, which previously surrounded more modest buildings.

BISHOP'S PALACE ILL. 14

1887—1894 • Episcopal Palace in Astorga, León

Joan Baptista Grau, whom Gaudí had already met while working for the Jesus and Mary Congregation, was appointed Bishop of Astorga in 1886. When the episcopal palace burnt down shortly afterwards, Gaudí was entrusted with the design of a new building. He was already very busy with other contracts, and the distances he was required to travel did not improve matters and resulted in numerous delays. In 1893 the bishop died and Gaudí designed the hearse and the headstone, before terminating the contract, since the client's payments were in arrears. At the time, at least the chapel was already completed. In the end, Gaudí's plans were finally implemented and work was completed in 1960.

KHAPLAIN'S HOUSE AND WORKSHOP ILL. 15

1887—1912 • Service building at the Sagrada Familia in Barcelona

From a very early stage in the construction of the Sagrada Familia, it became necessary to put up an additional building for those working on the technical and clerical sides of the project. Gaudí designed a simple structure with a small bell tower. The upper floor was the chaplain's living quarters, and there were also a design studio and model shop. Worth noticing is the sign in large letters suggesting that public transport passed this way.

COLEGIO TERESIANO ILL. 16
1888—1890 • Teresian Convent in Calle de Ganduxer, 85–105 in Barcelona
Founded by Father Enric d'Ossó i Cervelló in 1876, the Order of St Teresa was seeking a building in Barcelona as the order's headquarters where novice nuns could be trained. This meant that a girls' boarding school would form part of an extensive building program. As was the case with the Sagrada Familia, another architect had begun the work and Gaudí took over after the laying of the foundation stone, firstly designing the façade and then the whole building according to the existing floorplan. Pointed arches are seen throughout the compact three-storey building, but these are parabolic rather than Gothic arches. They accentuate the entrance and create an uplifting atmosphere in the corridors. The courtyards lend the building astonishing brightness.

CASA BOTINES
1891—1894 • Casa Fernández y Andrés, Plaza Obispo Don Marcelo in León
The statue of St George, Catalonia's patron saint, above the entrance to this neo-Gothic building with its rusticated limestone masonry, quickly and clearly reveals the loyalty to their homeland of Simón Fernández and Mariano Andrés, who together commissioned the work. The ground floor and basement were devoted to their textile business, while the two proprietors' apartments were situated on the first floor, with rented apartments on the two storeys above. With the small windows of the rented properties, the eye-catching corner turrets, the crenellated design of gabled dormer windows and the spiked railings surrounding

it, the building recalls a siege castle, an edifice standing alone, next to the Palacio de los Guzmanes, which although smaller in size only just fits into the space.

SPANISH FRANCISCAN MISSIONS ILL. 17
1892—1893 • Building for the Spanish Franciscan Missions in Tangiers
Commissioned by the Marquis of Comillas, for whose father Gaudí had already worked, the architect drew up plans for a large missionary church for the Franciscan Order. Gaudí went to stay with the Marquis for several months. The floorplan shows a square with rounded corners where the school and residential buildings surround the central chapel, above which 13 towers rise. Since no scale is indicated on the surviving drawings, it is difficult to estimate their height, although the plans seem to suggest that the tallest spire would have been slightly higher than the planned 164 feet. Despite their much smaller size, the towers are very similar to those of the Sagrada Familia.

COMILLAS SUMMER HOUSE
1893 • Rebuilding of the Comillas summer house at the Finca Güell
Because the small summer house, built to welcome the royal visit to Comillas was no longer needed, the estate workers pulled it down and moved it to Barcelona. When it reappeared a year later, many of the components, most notably the fabric roof cover, were no longer in use. Preparing to put the new summer house on show in the Finca Güell gardens, Gaudí designed what was essentially a new structure, although he did reuse the slightly raised platform.

ROOFTOP STRUCTURES
1894—1897 • Small projects for Eusebio Güell
In the 1890s, Gaudí worked on several small projects for Eusebio Güell at some of the latter's many real estate properties. These

14

15

16

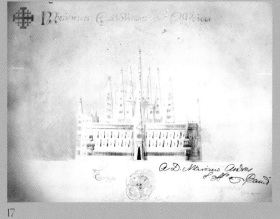

17

THE COMPLETE WORKS

included drawings for some temporary roofing on Paseo de Colón, housing for a water tank on the roof of Calle de Lancaster 7, a caretaker's apartment on the roof of Calle de Comte de l'Assalt 9, and laundry facilities on the roofs of Rambla de los Capuchinos 30 and Calle de Còdols 16. It is uncertain whether Gaudí was content with taking on small routine household jobs, but for friends he was willing to sign plans in the capacity of licensed architect, even when he played no part in carrying out or even preparing designs for a job.

BODEGAS GÜELL ILL. 18

1897—1900 • Bodegas Güell in Garraf

This building was attributed to Gaudí but in actual fact Francisco Berenguer was responsible for its construction. In any case, the plans were signed by Gaudí, while site management was down to his colleague and his co-workers. It is difficult to credit Francisco Berenguer with the design in all its complexity and vitality, since there are numerous elements and above all the compositional freedom that can only be found in Gaudí's work. However, the lack of colour and detail in the decorative design is hardly surprising as Gaudí himself was never to be seen on site.

CASA CALVET

1898—1904 • House on Calle de Caspe, 48 in Barcelona

Like Casa Botines, this building on Calle de Caspe in Barcelona's Eixample neighbourhood provides multifunctional space, with Calvet's textile business on the ground floor and in the basement and four residential apartments on upper floors. The ceiling above the ground floor extends well into the courtyard, creating a terrace for the apartment above. The smooth-faced façade, unlike that of the building in León, owes more to baroque rather than Gothic design, with relatively little emphasis on the bay windows and decorated gables. The large entrance hall, much needed by the textile business on the ground floor – only in the middle is there space reserved for access to the apartments – creates visual conflict with the large area of wall above. By placing four round pilasters up against it, Gaudí cleverly solved the problem.

GÜELL COLONY CRYPT

1898—1914 • Church for the Colonia Güell in Santa Coloma de Cervelló

Beginning in 1890 Eusebio Güell set about constructing a new textile factory in Santa Coloma de Cervelló. He also wanted to build a housing development for the workers, which at that time was not unusual and even necessary. Of course, the development included a chapel. When this proved to be too small, Gaudí was awarded the contract to build a church. However, by that time Gaudí was involved with numerous other assignments and was also engaged in a pilot scheme for the Sagrada Familia. When Güell fell ill in 1914, his children took over ownership of the development, cooperation ceased and Gaudí withdrew from the project, for which only the crypt had been completed.

TORRE BELLESGUARD

1900—1909 • House for Jaume Figueras on Calle de Bellesguard, 16–20 in Barcelona

The former summer residence of King Martin the Humane had fallen into disrepair after the monarch's death. It acquired the name, Bellesguard – *Beautiful View* – because it overlooked both city and sea. The ruins belonged to Bishop Joan Baptista Grau, for whom Gaudí had already designed the episcopal palace in Astorga, which was sold after the bishop's death in 1893. Gaudí managed to persuade the new owner, Maria de Sagués i Molins, widow of Jaume Figueras, to remodel the property as an elegant country house. The building stands on a more or less square ground plan crowned with a tower and the four-armed cross so typical of Gaudí's work, while exposed masonry on the house was produced from stones quarried nearby. Around the edges of the land surrounding the house, numerous ruins left standing were integrated into the new overall design, Gaudí only worked on the project until 1902. It was then completed by Domènec Sugrañes. He was responsible for the benches decorated with mosaics at the front of the house, the fountain and also the design of the staircase.

THE FIRST GLORIOUS MYSTERY OF THE ROSARY

1903—1907 • Design for the first shrine of the Monumental Rosary of Montserrat

Close to the Monastery of Montserrat is a footpath leading to a miraculous image of the Virgin Mary. The path was designed as a monumental rosary devoted to the 15 so-called mysteries, which together make up the five joyous events of the Annunciation and Childhood of Christ, the five agonising episodes of the Passion and the five glorious moments following the Resurrection. Gaudí created the representation of the first glorious mystery, the Resurrection, arranging a series of statues, carved by the sculptors Josep Llimona i Bruguera and Dionís Renart i Garcia, in a naturally occurring grotto in the mountainside, completed by the words *resurrexit, non est hic – He is not here; for he is risen.*

GÜELL PARK ILL. 19

1900—1914 • Calle de Olot in Barcelona

Eusebi Güell had found Ebenezer Howard's book about the concept of a garden city so interesting that he contemplated creating something similar on a vast hillside plot near Barcelona. Unfortunately, none of Gaudí's plans for the proposed development survive, but clearly the project was intended to attract the interest of wealthier members of the population. In the event, they showed no such interest. It is unclear whether it was because no one liked the designs for the house or because it was difficult for traffic to tackle the steep hill. In any case, the project was abandoned in 1914. The features of the park completed by then included a residential house that Gaudí himself later took up residence in, the park gate and two gatehouses, a wall overlooking the city as well as numerous paths and the hypostyle hall, originally intended as a market hall, with its roof terrace.

CAFÉ TORINO ILL. 20

1900—1902 • Tiles and interior design for Café Torino in Barcelona

The fact that Gaudí never touched alcohol did not prevent him from being involved in the design of a bar on Paseo de Gracia, which was to become a licensed premises best known for its Martinis. The client was Flaminio Mezzalama from Turin, who represented the vermouth producers Martini Rossi in Spain and wanted to create an attention-grabbing bar in the city. To carry out the work he hired the interior designer Ricard de Capmany i Roura and the architects Josep Puig, Pere Falqués i Urpí and Antoni Gaudí. As the latter had done at the Casa Vicens, for what became known as the Arabian Lounge, he covered the walls with tiles made of pressed and varnished cardboard manufactured at Hermenegildo Miralles i Anglès's factory. Visitors also found themselves surrounded by Venetian mosaics and Viennese furniture. The bar closed down in 1911.

CASA PERE SANTALÓ

1900 • Renovation of a façade on Nou de la Rambla in Barcelona

Pere Santaló i Castellví was, like Antoni Gaudí, a member of Asociación Catalanista de Excursiones Científicas (Catalan Scientific Excursions Association), a society which organised excursions to famous buildings in Catalonia. The two men met and in 1888 Gaudí helped his friend with the construction of stables on Calle de Córcega in the Gràcia district. In 1900, Pere Santaló moved to a new house on Nou de la Rambla, still known at the time as Comte de l'Assalt. Gaudí oversaw the renovation, which he kept extremely simple.

19

20

THE COMPLETE WORKS

21

22

FINCA MIRALLES ILL. 21

1902 • Wall and gate for the Finca Miralles in Barcelona

The industrialist Hermenegildo Miralles commissioned the architect Domènec Sugrañes to build a villa on his newly acquired estate, while Gaudí oversaw the construction of the external wall on the street side and the entrance gate. The wall with its undulating surface was topped by metal edging held up by curved joists.

CASA CASTELLDOSRIUS

1901—1903 • Refurbishment of a private house in Barcelona

Gaudí is believed to have created a variety of decorative elements for the renovation; however, no related drawings survived.

CHALET DE CATLLARÀS

1902—1904 • Chalet de Catllaràs in La Pobla de Lillet

The building was an apartment block for engineers from an out-of-the-way coalmine supplying Eusebi Güell's cement works, which traded as Asland, in Clot del Moro. Two apartments shared the three floors of the building, whose roof extends across the two curves that formed the barrel-vault structure, thanks to which each apartment was lit by mansard windows. The semi-circular floorplan of the proposed staircase on the longitudinal side provided sufficient space for two bathrooms on both first and second floor, a laundry room, a storeroom and a coal cellar. The usable space in the apartments varied considerably due to the shape of the building. While on the top floor there were two studio apartments, those on the floor immediately below had four rooms each. On the ground floor were four servants' rooms and two kitchens.

SANCTUARY OF THE MISERICORDIA ILL. 22

1903—1904 • Redesigning a church façade in Reus

Gaudí produced a new design for the west front of the church with a representation of the Virgin Mary as a shepherdess. The drawings suggest a baroque style with a triangular pediment and volutes on either side. The plan was never implemented, probably due to the high cost of the work and disputes between the potential clients. In the end, a new design by the architect Pere Caselles i Tarrats was finally chosen.

PALMA CATHEDRAL

1903—1914 • Restoration work in the Cathedral of Palma de Mallorca

Some time around 1900 Pere Joan Campins i Barceló, Bishop of Mallorca, contemplated introducing a new, improved, liturgically appropriate style for his cathedral. Gaudí's solution was to relocate the choir from the middle of the nave – where it blocked worshippers' view of the altar – to a side aisle, to improve the acoustics, and redesign the altar. A sumptuous baldachin, in whose creation Josep Maria Jujol played a major role, replaced the existing Gothic and baroque retablos. Other completed works were new stained-glass windows and several small pieces of furniture.

CHALET GRANER ILL. 23

1904 • Design for a house in Sant Gervasi de Cassoles

It was for the painter, Lluís Graner i Arrufí, that Gaudí made sketches for a house to be built on a site in Sant Gervasi de Cassoles. Apart from the fence, the entrance and the foundation, no work could be completed. Again, the client's financial means were insufficient to pay for the project. The surviving sketches are extremely promising. Here, Gaudí would have had the chance to apply the design vocabulary he had developed for Casa Batlló, this time not just

for the conversion of an existing building, but
for a completely new construction. The broad
sweep of the structural shell is accentuated by
a soaring tower, while the irregular but carefully thought-out curves of the roof and walls
can be observed from all sides.

LA SALA MERCÈ

**1904 · An entertainment venue
on the Rambla de Canaletas in Barcelona**
The same year in which Gaudí produced a
design for a house for Lluís Graner saw the ar-
rival of a movie theatre on Barcelona's Rambla
de Canaletas. Gaudí's contribution was probably confined to decorating the small audito-
rium. Graner worked on the project with [the
actor and director] Adrià Gual i Queralt and together they opened with the usual live music
and a show all about Montserrat. Movies and
theatrical performances were specifically presented as what one critic described as dream
visions. Later, *Grutas Fantásticas* (Fantastic
caverns), a cave-like exhibition space, was
set up in the basement for various dioramas,
for which Gaudí made a series of stalactites
and stalagmites. As well as representations
of a volcano or a waterfall, the ever-changing
succession of props also included religious
imagery. Graner extended his activities to another venue, but it was a failure which left its
impresario bankrupt. The Sala Mercè became
a conventional cinema.

ESTACIÓN DE FRANCIA

**1904 · Station building for Ferrocarriles de
Madrid a Zaragoza y Alicante**
The Compañía de los Ferrocarriles de Madrid
a Zaragoza y Alicante (MZA) asked Gaudí to
carry out a survey of the Barcelona terminus
which had been in service since 1848 and
now lacked sufficient space. Gaudí suggested
improving traffic flow by way of a terminal
loop, so that locomotives did not have to be
switched, as well as a new train shed roof.
The roof was built later but according to the
engineers' suggestion of a three-hinged arch,

rather than Gaudí's unusual tent construction
with pre-stressed beams.

TALLERES BADÍA ILL. 24

**1904 · Workshop in the Calle de Nápoles
in Barcelona**
José and Luís Badía were artisan blacksmiths
who had already filled a number of orders for
Gaudí when he designed a workshop for them.
The work was unusual in as much as Gaudí
had completely rejected all ornamentation,
but his distinctive style could still be seen
from the curved lines of the main frontage, as
well as in his decision to construct the building in stone, all of which follows the elegant
simplicity of the Obrera MatARONens without
achieving its grandeur. Gaudí took on the project in exchange for blacksmithing services by
his clients.

POMARET BRIDGE

**1904—1906 · Project for a viaduct over the
Pomaret River**
In 1904 a group of Sarrià residents demanded
the construction of a bridge across one of
the very deeply carved valleys north-west of
Barcelona, in order to connect the separate
ends of the Calle de la Inmaculada (known at
the time as Calle de Santa Eulalia) not far from
Torre Bellesguard. Because the city fathers
did not react, they approached Gaudí directly.
This unused design for a bridge 492-feet-
long as a piece of still-innovative concrete
construction manifests some surprising ideas.
The bridge piers are staggered, and the plan
shows the bridge following a wavy line and
the undulating, bricked-up parapets decorated with mosaics adorned with words which
could probably be interpreted as symbolising
Parc Güell's surrounding wall: *Per nosaltres
pregueu santa Eulàlia; pregueu per nosaltres –
Pray for us, St Eulalia, pray for us.*

23

24

25

26

CASA BATLLÓ ILL. 25

1904–1906 · Reconstruction of Casa Batlló in Barcelona

Like Casa Calvet, Casa Batlló is a large, inner-city apartment building, where the builder-proprietor and textile manufacturer Josep Batlló himself had his main residence. The original building, unrecognisable after Gaudí's reconstruction, was the work of one of his professors at the school of architecture. The façade, with its very subtle undulations, spreads across every floor as far as the scaled roof, on which perches a small tower topped by one of Gaudí's typical four-armed crosses. It also serves to mark the boundary with the house next door, Casa Amatller. Inside, the atrium designed as a source of light runs upwards through the building, so that colours of the walls, pale on the lower levels, turn darker as they travel towards the light. Another special feature is the ventilation system which Gaudí contrived specially for the building.

VIADUCT AT BELLESGUARD ILL. 26

1906–1908 · Construction of a viaduct in Barcelona

The new boundary wall between the historic corner towers, found to be necessary during work on the Bellesguard site, cut off an existing footpath leading up the mountain. In order for the route to be placed at a safe distance from the nearby stream, Gaudí designed a viaduct which, like the similar construction in Parc Güell, was set on ten slanting circular pillars along the line of the slope. The basic brick construction was covered by a layer of natural stone masonry so that it harmonised with the landscape.

THE ARTIGAS GARDENS ILL. 27

1905—1906 · Gardens of Can Artigas in La Pobla de Lillet

Joan Artigas i Alart, a textile manufacturer and friend of Güell's, asked Gaudí to design the grounds of his home in La Pobla de Lillet on the banks of the River Llobregat. The layout of the ground made the rushing waters of the little river its focal point, taking in two bridges, two fountains, a cave around the spring of magnesian water and a picnic area. Typical of the design are structures completely covered with pebbles, as is the case with the realistic sculptures scattered across the site. They include an eagle's head, the heads of men and women, and the heads of a lion and an ox adorning the fountains. Soon after work began, the client died and the project came to a standstill, the gardens running wild until they were restored in 1992.

LA PEDRERA ILL. 28

1905—1910 · Casa Milà, Paseo de Gracia, 92 and Calle de Provenza, 261–265 in Barcelona

While Casa Batlló still had to be fitted into the perimeter block development, when it came to the much larger Casa Milà – known as La Pedrera, or stone quarry – with its 1,939 square yard floorplan and six main storeys at the junction between Calle de Provenza and Paseo de Gracia, Gaudí could work with greater flexibility. A modern steel skeleton introduced into the stone apartment block framework enabled the construction of spacious and well-lit interiors. Access to the building was via two atriums and three entrances – one for motor vehicles making their way down to the underground garage – then, as now, a popular feature. The culmination of the construction process was to have been a 15-feet group of figures of the Virgin Mary and the Archangels Michael and Raphael, sculpted by Carles Mani i Roig, who also worked on the Sagrada Familia. They were not completed as the client did not approve. Gaudí's new associate Josep María Jujol designed the rather more appealing balcony rails.

MONUMENT TO KING JAMES I THE CONQUEROR

1907 · Monument in Barcelona

In preparation for the 700th anniversary of the birth of the Aragonese King Jacob I – King James I the Conquerorin Catalan – in 1908, there were plans to erect a monument to him near Barcelona Cathedral. Invited to submit drawings, Gaudí was not content with designing a monument and suggested that within the framework of the construction of the Vía Layetana, the monument could stand on a newly built city square. He went so far as to consider the form the façades of buildings on the square might take. Although the plans never came to fruition, a new square was later built at the same location, this time in honour of Ramon Berenguer III the Great.

SAGRADA FAMILIA SCHOOLS ILL. 29

1908—1913 · Parochial School

When building began, it was already clear that, as construction of the church progressed, the school project would at some point get in the way. Even so, the dismantling and relocation of the little school long after the turn of the 21st-century millennium amounted to a loss. Like none other of his works, it clearly expressed Gaudí's ideas on construction. Here, he could transfer elements of the natural world into architecture, free from any decorative elements. One example is the shape of the roof, which despite its undulating shape can be identified as a ruled surface, which means that it could be built on straight girders revolving around a central axis. There was room under this roof for 150 children to be accommodated in three classrooms, each with a tiny courtyard and its own fountain.

LA MIRANDA ILL. PAGE 470

1906—1907 · A tower for Damià Mateu in Llinars del Vallès

The industrialist and co-owner of Hispano-Suiza, Damià Mateu i Bisa, commissioned Gaudí to build a pavilion on the edge of his property in Llinars, to create a refuge for his wife where, as the story goes, she could meet with women friends or practise typically feminine craft skills. Gaudí, again working closely with Francesc Berenguer, devised a tower which could been seen for miles around. Beside the tower was a garden wall built out of cobbles, to which was fixed netting, instead of a chain-link fence, similar to that at Finca Miralles. In 1939 the family moved, the tower was demolished in 1962 and its latticework transferred to Parc Güell.

FINCA BELLESGUARD ILL. 30

1907 · Development and building project for Finca Bellesguard

In 1907, a large area of the land belonging to Finca Bellesguard was due to be used for urban development. On the instructions of the Figueras family, Gaudí drew up a plan for the development of a service road whose many twists and turns extended across the hilly plot of land and connected both sides to the existing roads. The plans were never carried out, no doubt because Gaudí's construction project had plunged the family into financial ruin.

HOTEL ATTRACTION ILL. 31

1908—1909 · Multipurpose building in New York

When in 1908 two visitors from New York asked Gaudí to design a building in New York City, the architect really had little time for such a commission. Nevertheless, a few drawings, albeit penned by his assistant Juan Matamala, have survived. They show a building with apartments, restaurants and spaces for cultural activities. One cross-section is clearly recognisable as

27

28

29

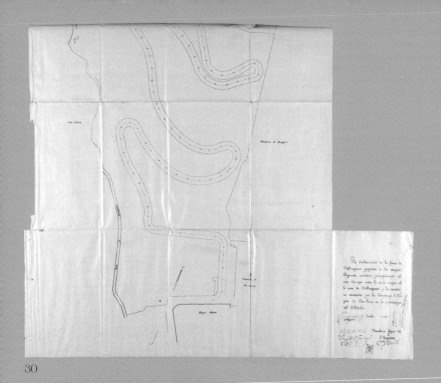

30

31

a theatre or movie house. Above, there is a gigantic, multistorey space in the upper part of the paraboloid, whose use is hard to guess. As is often the case with these sketches, the scale is somewhat unclear, the quoted height of 1,181 feet is seemingly no more reliable than the description of the building as a hotel. In any case, the plans were never put into practice.

STREET LAMPS ILL. 32
1910 • Street lamps in Vic
While recovering from illness and convalescing in the small town of Vic, Gaudí became involved in designing a memorial for the theologian Jaime Balmes y Urpía. His suggestion to create a memorial in the form of large street lamps was well received. Set on a pedestal of basalt blocks, the lamps were wrought-iron structures with four arms, from which the lanterns hung like fruit from a tree. At the top of each lamppost was the four-armed cross. The work was carried out by Josep María Jujol and José Canaleta Cuadras. In 1924 the lamps were taken down.

PULPITS ILL. 33
1912 • Pulpits for the parish church of Santa María in Blanes
Gaudí designed and built two hexagonal pulpits in the parish church of Santa María in Blanes. The work was commissioned by the journalist, Joaquim Casas i Carbó. The pulpit on the right side of the church was decorated with images of the Four Evangelists and crowned with a white dove symbolising the Holy Ghost. On the left side, four Apostles took the places of the Evangelists. Both pulpits were lost in a fire in 1936 amid the turmoil of the Spanish Civil War.

TORRAS I BAGES MONUMENT
1916 • Design for a memorial in Barcelona
The Bishop of Vic, Josep Torras i Bages, and Gaudí were interconnected by their shared support of a strongly religious Catalan nationalist movement. It was for this reason that Gaudí planned to erect a towering monument in front of the Sagrada Familia's Passion Façade. In 1916, Gaudí immediately commissioned the sculptor Juan Matamala Flotats to carve a bust, but it was destroyed in a fire in the studio in 1936. It was precisely this bust that was to be incorporated into the memorial. Attempts are currently under way to build the monument with the help of recent drawings, although those bear little resemblance to the single surviving sketch in Gaudí's hand.

PRAT DE LA RIBA MONUMENT
1917—1918 • Design for a monument in Castellterçol
Enric Prat de la Riba i Sarrà was the first president of the Commonwealth of Catalonia – Mancomunidad de Cataluña – a federation of the four Catalan provinces. Although it had no real authority, the alliance did play a vital role as the mouthpiece for those supporting the cause of regional identity. As a representative of a politically driven nationalist movement, he had been an opponent of Bishop Torres i Bages, who spoke for Catalan Catholic nationalism. Following Prat de la Riba's death in 1917, Gaudí outlined a plan for a monument to stand in the latter's birthplace, Castellterçol. At first, the idea was not made public, but some months later Lluís Bonet i Garí took over and unsuccessfully attempted to implement it. It is impossible to say how many of Bonet's surviving drawings were exactly the same as Gaudí's sketches and what changes Bonet made.

COLONIA CALVET

1923 · Chapel for the Colonia Calvet in Torelló

Little is known about plans to build a chapel for the cotton-spinning mill in Torrelló, which never progressed beyond a few drawings. The factory frequently changed ownership and the Calvets attempted some ambitious further developments, but their interest in the business came to an end in 1930 when the Ymbern family took over.

32

BIOGRAPHY

Photo from Gaudí's identification card at the World Exposition in Barcelona in 1888.

1852 Gaudí is born on 25 June in Reus, near Tarragona. His parents are Francesc Gaudí i Serra and Antònia Cornet i Bertran.

1863–1868 Gaudí attends secondary school in the Colegio de los Padres Escolapios, a monastic school in Reus.

1867 Gaudí publishes his first drawings in the *El Arlequin* newspaper, distributed in handwritten copies in Reus (in an edition of 12 copies). Gaudí draws backdrops for school plays.

1869–1874 Gaudí attends preparatory courses in order to be eligible to study architecture at the Faculty of Natural Science at Barcelona University.

1870 He designs the coat of arms for the Abbot of Poblet Monastery during restoration work on the building.

1873–1877 Gaudí studies architecture at the Escuela Provincial de Arquitectura in Barcelona. During his studies he makes numerous drafts, among others the design for a cemetery gate, a central hospital for Barcelona and a landing stage for ships. During his time at university, Gaudí spends his time working in architectural studios in order to earn money – for example, under Josep Fontseré and Francisco de Paula del Villar, who is later to start the Sagrada Familia project. Gaudí and Villar work together with others on the building of the Montserrat monastery.

1876 Gaudí's mother dies.

1878 Shortly before finishing his studies, Gaudí is awarded his first public contract. He is commissioned to design street lights for the city of Barcelona, the first of which are installed in 1879. On 15 March Gaudí receives his architect's diploma. Gaudí designs the windows for Esteve Cornelia, a glove merchant. Eusebi Güell is so taken with the window that he first becomes aware of Gaudí's work. At the same time, Gaudí works intensively on a project for the workers' cooperative settlement in Mataró. The project is on display at the World Exhibition in Barcelona. After completing his studies, Gaudí goes on trips with the Asociación de Arquitectos de Cataluña and the Asociación Catalanista de Excursiones Científicas in the vicinity of Barcelona in order to study old buildings. Gaudí is commissioned by Manuel Vicens to design an apartment building.

1879 Gaudí's sister, Rosita Gaudí de Egea, dies.

1881 Gaudí publishes an article on a craft exhibition in the daily paper, *La Renaixença*. It is Gaudí's only piece of journalism. The plans had meanwhile taken shape for the Mataró workers' settlement. They were printed by the Jepús bookprinters and were signed by Gaudí.

1882 Gaudí works closely with the architect Joan Martorell and, through the latter's agency, comes into close contact with neo-Gothic architecture.

1883 He takes on a project designing a hunting pavilion for Eusebi Güell in Garraf (near Sitges). On 3 November, Gaudí, at Martorell's suggestion, succeeds Villar on the Sagrada Familia project.

1883–1888 Gaudí works on the Casa Vicens, starts designing *El Capricho*, a country house in Comillas (near Santander) for Máximo Díaz de Quijano. As Gaudí continues to spend most of his time in Barcelona, he delegates supervision of the building work to the architect Cristóbol Cascante Colom.

1884–1887 Gaudí builds the entrance way and the stables for the Güell estate in Les Corts. This is his first major work for Güell.

1886–1889 Gaudí builds a town palace for Güell in Barcelona. During work on this project he travels, accompanied by the second Margrave of Comillas, through Andalusia and Morocco – a sign of his growing fame.

1887–1893 Gaudí builds the Bishop's Palace in Astorga.

1888–1889 Gaudí works on the Colegio Teresiano.

1891–1892 The Casa Botines is built in León. At the same time, Gaudí travels to Malaga and Tangier in order to study the site for the planned Franciscan Mission that he is supposed to design.

1893 The Bishop of Astorga dies. Gaudí designs a hearse for his patron's funeral and the ledger for the grave; he abandons work on the Bishop's Palace owing to increasing disagreement between himself and the episcopal authorities.

1894 Gaudí fasts too stringently during Lent showing how strongly religious he has by now become, whereas in earlier days he used to be somewhat cool towards religion.

1895–1901 Gaudí, together with his friend Francesc Berenguer, constructs a set of wine cellars for Güell in Garraf (near Sitges). For many years, Gaudí's hand in the project remained unknown.

1898 Gaudí starts work on the plans of the church in the Güell Colony. Although the

Antoni Gaudí's family home in Riudoms (Tarragona).

project drags on until 1916, it leaves a highly incomplete building behind: Gaudí built only the crypt and the entrance portal of the planned church.

1898–1900 Gaudí builds the Casa Calvet in Barcelona. In 1900, the city awards him the prize for the best building of the year. This is the only public award Gaudí ever receives.

1900 Gaudí is commissioned to design the first Glorious Secret of the Rosary for a large Rosicrucian project in the Montserrat Monastery.

1900–1909 On the grounds of the former country house of Martí, Gaudí builds a country house for Maria Sagués in the style of a mediaeval castle. The building is on a slope above Barcelona and received its name *Bellesguard* from the good view it afforded.

1900–1914 In 1900, Gaudí commences work on Güell's most ambitious project, namely, to build a large park and housing settlement in Gràcia (at the time on the outskirts of Barcelona). Only two of the houses planned were actually built, at the entrance to the grounds. Up until 1914 Gaudí spends time designing the entrance way, the large terrace or square and the complex network of paths and roads.

1901 Gaudí constructs a perimeter wall and entrance gate for Miralles, a factory owner.

1903–1914 Gaudí restores Palma Cathedral in Mallorca, and attempts to recreate the old liturgical meaning which was originally given to the interior of the cathedral.

1904–1906 Gaudí undertakes alterations to the apartment block owned by Josep Batlló in Barcelona. The result is an adventurous style, revolutionary for the age.

1906 Gaudí moves into one of the houses in Güell Park in order to save his father having to climb stairs. His father dies on 29 October of the same year.

1906–1910 The Casa Milà is built – Gaudí's largest apartment house project.

1908 Gaudí is commissioned to build a hotel in New York. Things get only as far as draft design drawings, which reveal a daring constructional vision. In the same year, Gaudí plans to erect a chapel for the Colegio Teresiano. The project is dashed by disagreement between Gaudí and the Mother Superior of the convent. Work is started on building the Güell Colony Crypt in Santa Coloma.

1909 Gaudí builds the Sagrada Familia parish school.

1910 Numerous works of Gaudí's are shown at the Société Nationale de Beaux-Arts Exhibition in Paris. This is the only exhibition of Gaudí's work outside Spain to be held in his lifetime. Eusebi Güell is made a count.

1912 Gaudí's niece, Rosa Egea i Gaudí, dies at the age of 36.

1914 Gaudí's close friend and colleague, Francesc Berenguer dies; Gaudí had received his first schooling in Reus together with Francesc from the latter's father. Gaudí decides to devote all his attention to the Sagrada Familia.

1926 On 7 June Gaudí is hit by a tram while out walking. He dies three days later in the Hospital de la Santa Cruz in Barcelona.

FAR LEFT · On 12 June 1926, thousands lined the streets of Barcelona as the funeral procession with Gaudí's coffin passed by.

LEFT · In 1915, the papal nuncio Francesco Ragonesi visited the Sagrada Familia construction site, accompanied by the Bishop of Barcelona, Enrique Reig y Casanova.

PHOTO CREDITS

123RF — Sergi Reboredo: 351 r., 368; Mauro Rodrigues: 358; Jos Manuel Sanchez Guerrero: 217

akg-images — Album/Kurwenal/Prisma: 237; Album/Ramon Manent: 86, 114 b.; Album/Oronoz: 174; Album/Prisma: 190; Album/Miguel Raurich: 243; Manuel Cohen: 268–269; De Agostini Picture Library: 287

Alamy Stock Photo — 4k-Clips: 112–113; age fotostock: 184, 485 b. l.; Arcaid Images: 298; Cro Magnon: 176–177, 485 t.; Design Pics Inc.: 165; dleiva: 373; Dragomir Donchev: 446–447; Jon Mikel Duralde: 105; f8 images: 140–141, 142; Factofoto: 314; Jordi Sans Galitó: 87, 119; GM Photo Images: 257, 258–259; Tim Graham: 199; Susana Guzman: 91; Heritage Image Partnership Ltd.: 218; Mark Higham: 455; imageBROKER: 103, 224; iWebbtravel: 419; JHeinimann: 427; Jon Arnold Images Ltd.: 71; jordiphotography: 267; John Kellerman: 45, 344–345, 405, 420; Semen Lihodeev: 381; Bob Masters: 36; John McKenna: 384–385, 418; Hercules Milas: 143, 342; Leandro Mise: 317; Julian Money-Kyrle: 460–461; Panther Media GmbH: 166–167, 250–251, 254; Alberto Paredes: 170–171; Stefano Paterna: 360–361; Cisco Pelay: 452; Stefano Politi Markovina: 339; Prisma by Dukas Presseagentur GmbH: 72–73, 392–393; Jozef Sedmak: 423; Michal Sikorski: 388–389; Marc Soler: 306–307; Steven Allen Travel Photography: 332; Ferenc Ungor: 66; Lucas Vallecillos: 32–33, 61, 94–95, 106–107, 128, 162–163, 223, 395, 396–397, 398; Ivan Vdovin: 96, 245; Alvaro German Vilela: 200; Visions from Earth: 46; Washington Imaging: 30; Rob Whitworth: 442–443; Jan Wlodarczyk: 296–297; World History Archive: 504

Arxiu Dr. Cèsar Comas Llaberia: 27

Arxiu Fotogràfic de Barcelona: 219, 466 t.

Arxiu Mas, Fundació Institut Amatller D'Art Hispanic, Barcelona: 28–29, 39, 50, 62, 64–65, 83 b., 84–85, 110, 120, 148, 158–159, 161, 173, 196, 276, 293, 311, 333, 341, 362, 363, 364–365, 400–401, 406–407, 409, 432, 433, 434–435, 467, 477, 482, 485 m., 489 b., 490 t., 506

Arxiu Municipal de Barcelona: 227, 304–305, 366–367, 386, 390–391, 481 t. r., 498 t.

Author's archives: 494 b., 505

Bridgeman Images — De Agostini Picture Library: 236, 284, 290–291; Photo © Christie's Images: 239

David Cardelús/ARTUR IMAGES: 357, 369

F. Català-Roca, Barcelona: 35, 168, 194–195,
205 t., 231, 288, 403

Col·legi d'Arquitectes de Catalunya,
Barcelona: 410 l.

George R. Collins & Juan Bassegoda Nonell,
The Designs and Drawings of Antonio Gaudí,
Princeton, 1983: 300–301, 474 b. r., 490 b.

Carlos Flores, *Gaudí, Jujol, y el modernismo
catalan*, Madrid, 1982: 462–463

Elisabeth Galas, Cologne: 114 t., 115

Gaudí Chair, Barcelona School of Architecture,
Universitat Politècnica de Catalunya: 8,
10–11, 19, 20–21, 133 t., 152, 183, 192, 215,
232, 233, 238, 246, 249 b., 262, 289, 340,
415, 464–465, 474 b. l., 478 t., 485 b. r.,
493 b., 498 b., 501, 509

Getty Images — DEA PICTURE LIBRARY: 88–89;
José Fuste Raga: 264–265; Michelle
McMahon: 295; Roc Canals Photography:
253 t., 261

Peter Gössel, Bremen: 41, 83 t., 102 b., 111 t.,
172, 214, 376–377, 382

Reto Guntli, Zurich: 336–337

Timothy Hursley, Little Rock: 7

Institut d'Estudis Fotogràfics de Catalunya:
470

INTERFOTO/PHOTOAISA/Lucas Vallecillos: 191

The Interior Archive/Fritz von der Schulen-
burg: 146

Junta Constructora del Temple Expiatori de la
Sagrada Família, Barcelona: 49, 53, 248–
249, 416, 497 b.

Nicole Kuhlmann, Bremen: 205 b., 242, 253 b.,
292

Luca Locatelli/INSTITUTE: 57, 58–59

Antonio Lopez, *Barcelona á la vista. Album de
fotografías de la capital y sus alrededores*,
Barcelona, 1896: 474 t.

Museu de Montserrat: 473 b.

José F. Ráfols, *Antonio Gaudí*, Barcelona, 1929:
2, 466 b., 473 t., 478 b. l., 481 t. l., 493 t., 502

François René Roland: 175

Christian Schallert/Jordi Garcia, Barcelona: 42,
69, 70, 74, 75, 76, 77, 78, 79, 93, 99, 100, 101,
102 t., 109, 111 b., 117, 122–123, 125, 126–127,
130–131, 132, 133 b., 134, 135, 136, 139, 147,
151, 156, 160, 179, 180–181, 188, 207, 208–
209, 210, 211–212, 216, 220–221, 226, 228,
234, 240, 266, 271, 272, 274, 275, 279, 280,
282, 283, 303, 308, 312–313, 315, 318, 320,
327, 328, 329, 330, 335, 343, 346, 349, 350–
351, 352, 353, 354, 375, 378, 379, 410–411,
412, 414, 417, 424, 431, 436, 439, 440–441,
444, 448, 451, 456–457, 481 b., 486, 489 t.,
494 t., 497 t. l., 497 t. r.

Luca Schroeder, Frechen: 60, 90, 104, 118, 164,
178, 198, 206, 222, 244, 270, 294, 338, 372,
404, 458

© Keiichi Tahara, BUILT Ltd.: 144–145, 153,
154–155, 157, 263, 370–371, 413

ullstein bild — Werner Cohnitz: 24; IBERFOTO:
468–469; SZ Photo/Scherl: 23; TopFoto: 54

LEFT · The Corpus Christi procession in 1924 leaving the cathedral.
In the foreground is Antoni Gaudí
with other participants of the Cer-
cle Artístic de Sant Lluc. This circle
of artists was founded as a Catholic
moral reaction to the Real Círculo
Artístico de Barcelona, which was
committed to Catalan Modernism.

BIBLIOGRAPHY

It is almost impossible to give an overview of the literature on Antoni Gaudí. Initially, it was only his close friends who commented on his works and intentions. Soon, however, a veritable flood of publications was forthcoming, all concerned with the future-oriented aspects of Gaudí's oeuvre.

The present book should not be understood as another contribution to research already undertaken on Gaudí; it is supposed to introduce the reader to Gaudí and give them a flavour of Gaudí's work, perhaps encouraging them to travel to Spain (and you do not even have to travel around much, as most buildings can be found in Barcelona). The select bibliography below is intended to lay the basis for closer reading on Gaudí. The choice hinges on German publications or those relatively easy to obtain in Germany.

A general introduction to art nouveau, with a brief series of appraisals of Gaudí's work can be found in:
Sembach, Klaus-Jürgen: *Art Nouveau*. Cologne, 2016.

César Martinell's large Gaudí book is invaluable. Martinell spoke with numerous contemporaries of Gaudí and presents comprehensive material on the architect otherwise not available, especially since Gaudí himself hardly ever gave written statements on his work. One therefore has to rely on statements he made in conversation.
Martinell, Cèsar: *Antoni Gaudí* (Spanish edition: Barcelona, 1967; Italian ed.: Milan, 1955; English ed.: Barcelona, 1975).

Collins, George R.: *Antonio Gaudí*. Ravensburg, 1962.
Collins, George R.; Bassegoda Nonell, Juan: *The Designs and Drawings of Antoni Gaudí*. Princeton, 1983.
Crippa, Maria A.; Bergós Massó, Juan; Bassegoda Nonell, Juan: *Gaudí. Der Mensch und das Werk*. Ostfildern-Ruit, 2000.
Crippa, Maria A. (Ed.): *Gaudí. Interieurs, Möbel, Gartenkunst*. Ostfildern-Ruit, 2001.
Crippa, Maria A.: *Gaudí*. Cologne, 2015.
Dalisi, Riccardo: *Antonio Gaudí – Möbel und Objekte*. Stuttgart, 1981.
Flores, Carlos: *Gaudí, Jujol y el Modernismo Catalan*. Madrid, 1982.
Güell, Xavier: *Antoni Gaudí*. Zurich and Munich, 1987.
Permanyer, Luís: *Gaudí of Barcelona*. New York, 1996.
Ràfols, José F.: *Gaudí*. Barcelona, 1960 (3rd ed.).
Roe, Jeremy: *Antoni Gaudí*. New York, 2006.
Solà-Morales, Ignasi de: *Gaudí*. Stuttgart, 1983.
Sterner, Gabriele: *Barcelona: Antoni Gaudí y Cornet. Architektur als Ereignis*. Cologne, 1979.
Sweeney, James J.; and Sert, Josep L.: *Antonio Gaudí*. Stuttgart, 1960.
Wiedemann, Josef: *Antoni Gaudí. Inspiration in Architektur und Handwerk*. Munich, 1974.

RIGHT · In 1904, when working on the Monumental Rosary of Montserrat, Gaudí made a hike up the mountain. He can be seen here with his father, his niece and his friend Pere Santaló i Castellví.

MAP OF THE BUILDINGS

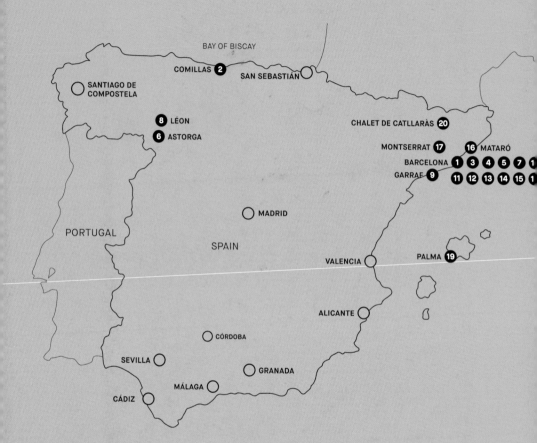

BAY OF BISCAY

COMILLAS **2** SAN SEBASTIÁN

SANTIAGO DE COMPOSTELA

8 LÉON

6 ASTORGA

CHALET DE CATLLARÀS **20**

MONTSERRAT **17** **16** MATARÓ

BARCELONA **1** **3** **4** **5** **7** **1**

GARRAF **9** **11** **12** **13** **14** **15** **1**

PORTUGAL

MADRID

SPAIN

VALENCIA

PALMA **19**

ALICANTE

CÓRDOBA

SEVILLA

GRANADA

MÁLAGA

CÁDIZ

1 Casa Vicens

2 El Capricho

3 Finca Güell

4 Sagrada Familia

5 Güell Palace

6 Bishop's Palace

7 Colegio Teresiano

8 Casa Botines

9 Bodegas Güell

10 Casa Calvet

11 Güell Colony Crypt

12 Torre Bellesguard

13 Güell Park

14 Casa Batlló

15 La Pedrera

16 La Obrera Mataronense

17 First Glorious Secret of the Rosary

18 Finca Miralles

19 Palma Cathedral

20 Chalet de Catllaràs

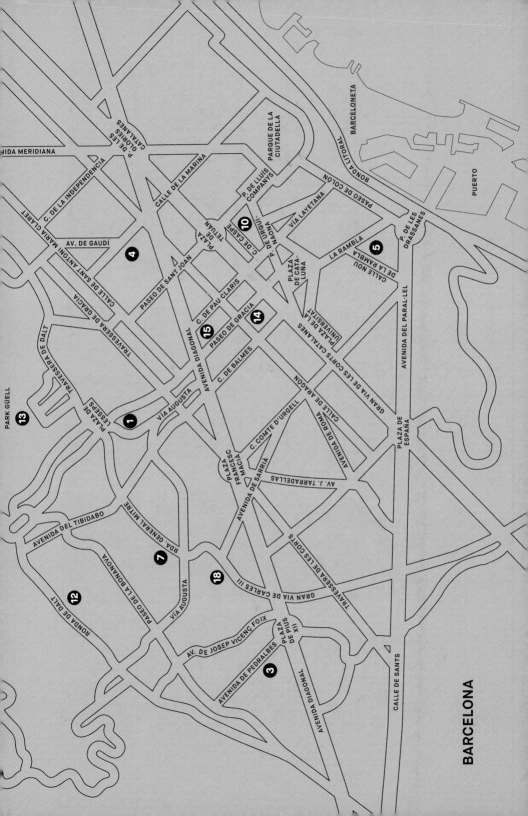

IMPRINT

This book could not have been written without the existence of its predecessors. In 1978 Rikuyo-sha published a two-volume work on the architecture of Gaudí – *Gaudí: Arte y Arquitectura*. The text for that work was written by Professor Joan Bassegoda i Nonell, holder of the Gaudí chair at the Universidad Politécnica de Cataluña. In 1985 Rikuyo-sha published a one-volume edition of his 1978 Gaudí work entitled *Gaudí: Arte y Arquitectura*, which constitutes the basis of this book. The publishers would like to thank all those concerned for their preliminary work.

COVER ·
Palacio Güell, Barcelona, 1886–1889
Photo: Christian Schallert/Jordi Garcia

BACK COVER ·
Sagrada Familia, Barcelona, 1883–1926
Photo: Alamy Stock Photo/Rob Whitworth

To stay informed about TASCHEN and our upcoming titles, please subscribe to our free magazine at www.taschen.com/magazine, follow us on Instagram and Facebook, or e-mail your questions to contact@taschen.com.

© 2022 TASCHEN GmbH
Hohenzollernring 53, D–50672 Köln
www.taschen.com

Original edition:
© 1987 Benedikt Taschen Verlag GmbH

Text: Dr. Rainer Zerbst
Updates, captions and catalogue of works:
  Peter Gössel
Project management: Jascha Kempe
Design: Anna-Tina Kessler and Birgit Eichwede
English translation: Doris Jones, Jeremy
  Gaines and Isabel Varea-Riley

Printed in Bosnia–Herzegovina
ISBN 978–3–8365–6619–3